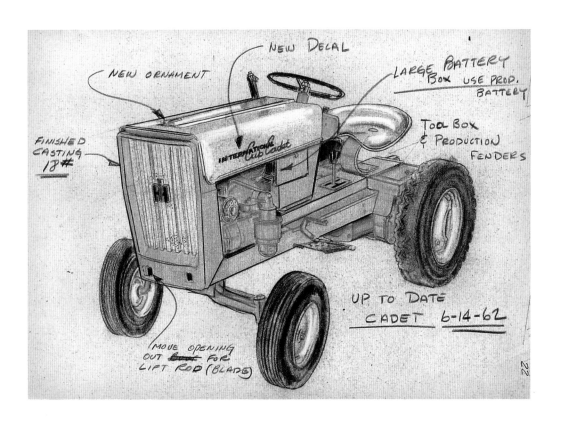

NEW DECAL

NEW ORNAMENT

LARGE BATTERY BOX USE PROD. BATTERY

TOOL BOX & PRODUCTION FENDERS

FINISHED CASTING 18#

UP TO DATE CADET 6-14-62

MOVE OPENING OUT ~~BACK~~ FOR LIFT ROD (BLADE)

22

GARDEN TRACTORS

*Deere, Cub Cadet,
Wheel Horse, and All the Rest,
1930s to Current*

BOLENS

By Oscar H. Will III

Voyageur Press

First published in 2009 by Voyageur Press, an imprint of MBI Publishing Company, 400 First Avenue North, Suite 300, Minneapolis, MN 55401 USA

Voyageur Press titles are also available at discounts in bulk quantity for industrial or sales-promotional use. For details write to Special Sales Manager at MBI Publishing Company, 400 First Avenue North, Suite 300, Minneapolis, MN 55401 USA.

To find out more about our books, visit us online at www.voyageurpress.com.

Library of Congress Cataloging-in-Publication Data

Will, Oscar H., 1956-
    Garden tractors : Deere, Cub Cadet, Wheel Horse, and all the rest, 1930s to current / Oscar H. Will III. -- 1st ed.
    p. cm.
ISBN 978-0-7603-3196-5 (plc)
1. Garden tractors. I. Title.
S711.W495 2009
631.3'72--dc22
          2008032755

Editor: Leah Noel
Designer: Elly Gosso
Cover designed by Koechel-Peterson and Associates, Inc., Minneapolis, MN

Printed in China

Cover illustration courtesy of the Wisconsin Historical Society (image 42055)

CONTENTS

This 1938 Shaw RD8 was a real workhorse in its day. The machine's engine made about eight horsepower at 2,500 rpm and could pull at least one eight-inch plow bottom, depending on the conditions.

CHAPTER 1

THE MARKET EMERGES
(PRE–WORLD WAR II)

In the United States, small, simple, light tractors specifically designed to handle the tasks of managing domestic gardens didn't become their own segment in the tractor market until after World War I, during which, ironically, the federal government made its first push for people to establish a War Garden and grow food for themselves and others. During this effort, folks with larger vegetable patches employed some smaller farm tools to till, plant, and weed the garden; most of these were still powered by animals, such as horses or mules. Those with smaller gardens turned to the age-old hoe, fork, and walking cultivator to keep their food production in order.

Indeed, companies like Brinly-Hardy survived the changes from horse to tractor farming by repurposing many of their products for the gardener, who by default used animal power or human power instead of petroleum power. Likewise, the S. L. Allen Company of Philadelphia continued to grow by producing a complete line of human-powered walking cultivators under the Planet Jr. label. These could be equipped with everything from a moldboard plow to a single-row seed planter.

Continued to page 10

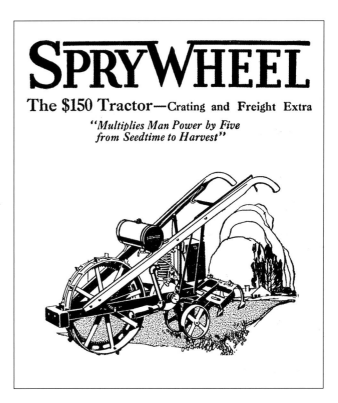

The H. C. Dodge Company of Boston, Massachusetts, produced this SpryWheel walking tractor in 1921 and 1922. The machine was typical of the walking tractors that were produced for many years. This model burned about a gallon of gasoline a day. *Author's collection*

THE FIRST
MOTORIZED PLOW

In 1915, Benjamin Franklin Gravely built what some historians say was the first motorized walking plow. He essentially grafted an Indian motorcycle engine to an existing wheel plow and created a machine that was cumbersome, but capable—especially when considering the alternative. The next year he obtained a patent on the device and went into business. By 1922, Gravely had amassed investors and capital sufficient to found the Gravely Motor Plow Company in Charleston, North Carolina.

For many years, Gravely offered only walking equipment, including the highly functional and collectible Model L two-wheeled tractor, which was released in 1937. As with all manufacturing companies of the day, Gravely produced very few walking tractors or other machines during World War II, except for those sold to the armed forces.

It wasn't until 1964 that the first Gravely 400 Series Winchester four-wheel tractor rolled off the assembly line. This machine was notable in that it looked very much like a conventional garden tractor except from the rear. Gravely adopted a rear-engine design that in no way resembled the open-frame Page and Allis-Chalmers G. Similarly oriented tractors were produced into the 1990s.

In 1982, Gravely, which was then owned by McGraw Edison Company, was purchased by Ariens and operated as a wholly owned subsidiary for many years. In 1992, Gravely production moved to Brillion, Wisconsin, and marketing and sales followed in 1997.

Today, a number of zero-turning-radius mowers, walk-behind mowers, and other equipment are offered as part of the Gravely brand.

Shaw Manufacturing's smallest four-wheel garden tractor offering, the Master Du-All, could be had with power ranging from three to eight horsepower at a cost of about $300 by the late 1930s. *Author's collection*

The Centaur Small Farm Tractor was typical of early riding versions of the larger walking tractors available in the early 1920s. Central Tractor Company of Greenwich, Ohio, manufactured this beast of a machine. *Author's collection*

GILSON AND BOLENS:
THE START OF A SUCCESSFUL PARTNERSHIP

In the 1850s, Theodore Gilson founded a small agricultural machine manufacturing company in Port Washington, Wisconsin. When his son John came of age and joined the business, his creative design talents were quickly put to work. In 1893, John invented a novel metal bracket that allowed office chairs to swivel and their backs to tilt. The importance of this device wasn't lost on the family, and shortly thereafter John left his dad's company and founded the Gilson Office Chair Company. Within three years, newspaperman and entrepreneur Harry Bolens joined forces with John Gilson, eventually becoming a financial partner and president of the company.

Sometime near the beginning of the second decade of the twentieth century, the Bolens name appeared on Gilson's products, and by 1914, Harry Bolens owned the chair-making company outright. By 1916, John Gilson and his son John Jr. had founded the J. E. Gilson Company, which produced among other things garden tools. Harry Bolens wisely bought into this company too, and soon the Gilson-Bolens collaboration was producing engines for the Beeman Garden Tractor Company of Minneapolis, Minnesota.

By the early 1920s, Gilson was selling garden tractors under the Bolens name. These tractors were followed by a series of mowers, power hoes, and other machines. Models came and went, but Bolens continued to refine the two-wheeled garden tractor for the next several decades. In the late 1920s, the company's name was changed to Gilson-Bolens, and some references report that the chair company was folded into the mix.

In 1939, Automated Products Company of Milwaukee acquired Gilson-Bolens and shortly changed its name to Bolens Products Division of the Automated Products Company. At the end of World War II, Automated was put up for sale but ultimately decided to upgrade its facilities when no buyers stepped forward. In 1946, the chair business was sold, and shortly after Food Machinery Corporation (FMC), looking for a place to build specialized tractors, snapped up Bolens along with its parent company. This marriage gave rise to the first true Bolens riding tractor, which was called the Ridemaster, in 1947.

FMC grew its Bolens Division with further research and development and an acquisition or two through the early 1980s. In 1982, employees purchased the Bolens Division to form Bolens Corporation, which was in turn purchased by Garden Way Inc. in 1988. After several prosperous years, the company was again sold in 2001—this time to MTD Consumer Group, Inc., of Cleveland.

Still, the Bolens name lives on in the capable hands of MTD and is sold almost exclusively through select home-improvement franchises.

Released shortly after World War II, the Bolens Huski Ridemaster was instrumental in drawing Food Machinery Corporation's interest in purchasing the tractor maker. Under FMC's ownership, several models of the Ridemaster were offered well into the 1950s.

9

The 1948 Osco was produced in Philadelphia and featured a fully automatic clutch and three-speed worm-gear drive. The 6.5-horsepower machine offered individual rear steering brakes and rack-and-pinion steering

Continued from page 7

By 1916, the year Benjamin Franklin Gravely patented his Gravely Motor Plow, small internal combustion engines were readily available, if not plentiful, all over the country. The prototype for Gravely's motor plow was built with parts obtained from a human-powered push plow and the engine from an Indian motorcycle. It was a little heavy and somewhat cumbersome, but it was a heck of a lot easier to turn the soil in a half-acre garden with that tool than the push plow it was based on. That same year, the Brillion Iron Works (established in Brillion, Wisconsin, by Henry and Christine Ariens) was busy kicking out castings of all kinds, and J. E. Gilson had amicably parted ways with Harry Bolens. Bolens and Gilson both played important roles in the garden tool business and collaborated on a two-wheeled gasoline-powered garden tractor, which was ready for sale in 1919.

By 1910, Sears, Roebuck and Company had purchased the David Bradley Manufacturing Company, a farm machinery maker, but the department store chain and catalog order company wouldn't release its first motor-powered walking tractor until the early 1930s. In 1921, Knud

ARIENS: A ROTARY TILLER SAVES THE DAY

The Brillion Iron Works—founded in Brillion, Wisconsin, in the late 1800s by Henry and Christine Ariens—declared bankruptcy in 1929 with the onset of the Great Depression but didn't cease operating entirely. It seems the company had designed, and was ready to produce, a rotary tiller unlike any other tilling machine available at the time. By 1933, this device, which was reportedly powered by a 14-horsepower four-cylinder gasoline-fueled engine, was the Ariens Rotary Tiller, and it was enough of a success that the family decided to spin off the Ariens brand in a separate company. This company would be run by Steve Ariens, the eldest son of the founders.

The production of tillers carried Ariens through World War II and kept the company alive afterwards. During the war, Ariens facilities focused on military strategic production. By the 1950s, the company had turned from its more commercial tiller focus to offering a complete lineup of upscale yard-care machines for the new wave of suburbanites. The company's most notable contribution during that time was probably the snow thrower, which is still available in a much-updated form today.

Ariens is still in business in the twenty-first century, as a privately held, family-owned company that has included acquisitions of the Sperry-New Holland line of garden tractors and Gravely over the years. Today, the company manufactures a wide range of outdoor power equipment, including snow throwers and zero-turning-radius mowers.

and Oscar Jacobsen of Racine, Wisconsin, decided to focus their manufacturing efforts on turf-maintenance machinery and shortly thereafter released the 4-Acre model, which they claimed was the first power mower designed specifically to cut turf. That same year, Shaw Manufacturing,

SPEEDEX:
HAROLD POND'S SUCCESSFUL LINE

Harold Pond founded his Speedex Tractor Company in 1935 in Ravenna, Ohio. That same year, the company came out with a tiller-steered garden tractor, the Model B Speedex. The tractor was assembled with a transmission from Ford's Model A and a narrowed rear axle from a Model T. The little machine was powered with Briggs & Stratton's Model ZZ air-cooled engine and is said to be the first four-wheel garden tractor with an air-cooled engine and pneumatic tires.

These early Speedex tractors have a typical late 1940s through 1950s tiller- or lever-steered look. Makers such as Economy, Beaver, and many others used a similar layout, but the components and frame structures were quite different.

The Model B was an immediate success and rapidly outsold the company's two-wheeled walking models. By 1948, Pond's business was thriving, so much so that Ford was no longer interested in selling him parts. Speedex quickly developed its own drivetrain and was never again dependent upon a potentially competitive supplier.

After a good 20 years of reasonable success, Pond sold Speedex to Maury Foote and Jerry Stowe in 1955. This unlikely pair (a potato farmer/teacher and a musician/road sign maker) took the brand to the next levels with continuous design refinements and better, more purposeful attachments. Under the new leadership, Speedex manufacturing reached about 1,000 units per year.

General Combustion Company of Alliance, Ohio, acquired Speedex in 1969 and continued to produce a modest number of machines annually, about 1,500. During the next three decades, the company was credited with offering the first fully floating mowing deck and the first diesel-powered garden tractor to be manufactured in the United States.

In 1997, Trans Tech International, Ltd., of New Philadelphia, Ohio, purchased Speedex. Replacement parts are still available through Trans Tech.

based in Galesburg, Kansas, was assembling small tractors using Ford automobile parts. These eventually led to the Shaw Du-All line of four-wheel riding tractors.

When the stock market crashed in 1929, all industries were hit hard—including the lawn and garden manufacturing industry. By then, scores of manufacturers were producing little walking tractors. Many of them went bankrupt, some consolidated into larger companies, and others simply survived. Like a phoenix rising from its own ashes, however, the lawn and garden industry rebounded after the Depression, when new innovation and ingenuity led to the development of more sophisticated garden tractors.

As might be expected, most of the post-Depression garden tractor development focused on two-wheel walking models. By the mid-1930s, these machines could be found with multispeed transmissions and all manner of attachments, including tillers, mowers, cultivators, planters, grader blades, and more. Some manufacturers had the brilliant idea to offer a trailing sulky attachment for their garden tractors, which would allow the operator to sit and ride behind the machine rather than walking. These simple attachments did much to transform consumers' expectations, but they didn't become ubiquitous, which speaks to their cumbersome nature and lack of maneuverability.

This high-clearance Gard'n Mast'r garden tractor was equipped with a mechanically powered tool lift that the company called the Roto-Lok.

In 1935, Harold Pond founded his Pond Tractor Company (Pond Garden Tractor Company in some references). Harold had worked in a number of capacities for Shaw Manufacturing and even represented Shaw in Ohio. He eventually found himself building his own Pond (soon to be known as Speedex) garden tractors, first in Alliance, Ohio, and later in Ravenna, Ohio. Harold made no bones about borrowing from the Shaw production model and scrounging parts from other manufacturers to assemble his own two-wheeled garden tractors. It would be a few years before he and his brother worked out the details of a functional four-wheel garden tractor.

Just two years later, in 1937, the Simplicity Manufacturing Company (based in Port Washington, Wisconsin) entered the two-wheeled garden tractor market with a highly successful line of walking tractors marketed through Montgomery Ward and Company. Simplicity's roots included a line of gasoline-fueled engines and even a couple of farm tractors. By 1939, Simplicity offered a sulky attachment to go with its fairly extensive lineup of two-wheeled tractors, but the manufacturer was not alone in that arena.

A few short years later, many heavy manufacturing companies, including most of those mentioned above, were diverted to producing materiel for World War II, or at the very least they were producing only a small fraction of the lawn and garden machines they had before-hand. The federal government's Victory Garden program, however, much like the War Garden program before it, did nothing but spur the public's desire to get back to gardening. By the time World War II was over, more folks than ever were ready to produce their own food.

It is doubtful that anyone knew it, but the lawn and garden industry was about to take off in North America, as people moved out to suburbia to tend their own little acre or fraction thereof. At the same time, farms were getting smaller and horses scarcer. Postwar America was ripe for a machinery revolution in many arenas, and in the garden tractor industry that revolution came on with full force.

LEFT: An up-close look at an original condition Gard'n Mast'r decal.
BELOW: The Garden-All Tractor Company of Liberty, Indiana, built four-wheeled machines like this one in the early 1950s. In many cases, the so-called Gard'n Mast'r garden tractor's drivetrain utilized Dodge truck components.

THE Gard'n Mast'r GARDEN TRACTOR

TOP LEFT: In 1953, Simplicity's lineup included four machines ranging in power from two to five horsepower and included a Model J self-propelled mower. *Author's collection*

TOP MIDDLE: The two-wheeled Red Flyer built by the Red-E Tractor Company was indicative of walking-tractor evolution in the early 1950s. This company also built a few four-wheeled models and is said to have had links to the maker of Economy and Power King tractors. *Author's collection*

TOP RIGHT: Roths Industries of Alma, Michigan, built several walking tractors and this steering wheel–equipped version called the BesRo Riding Tractor. The tractor was unusual because it used a single "guide wheel" on the sulky.

BOTTOM LEFT: This trade ad for the 1953 Pond Wheel Horse makes the claim that dealers will receive big profits from rapid sales of the tractor and brags that the entire Wheel Horse lineup is advertised in *Better Homes & Gardens* magazine. *Author's collection*

Introduced in the late 1950s, the Speedex Model S-14 was in the lineup for years. This beautifully restored example is a 1966 model.

CHAPTER 2

FOCUSING THE MARKET:
A POST–WORLD WAR II SCRAMBLE
(1946–1959)

While garden tractor manufacturers were cranking out goods to support the war effort in the 1940s, huge demand was building for all kinds of manufactured products back home. Once the military contracts dwindled down after the war's end, the pent-up demand for goods set off a spending frenzy that included everything from automobiles and appliances to trucks, tractors, and homes on the outskirts of cities. As GIs streamed back into the workforce, the entire population followed the American Dream right into suburbia. And as former farmlands were developed into neighborhoods, more and more homeowners wanted tools to help them keep their new lawns and gardens looking great. The demand was so great that existing garden tool manufacturers could barely keep up.

By some estimates, about 100 manufacturers of lawn and garden equipment existed at the time; yet, in reality, the number was likely much greater since ma and pa operations existed virtually everywhere. Some folks built machines from readily available materials and sourced engines from the major makers. Others offered more sophisticated machines and created stylized body panels from fiberglass and steel. Still others offered machines that were purposefully designed and built from the ground up.

At the same time, agricultural machinery makers were still trying to convince smaller farmers to trade in their draft animals for tractors after the war. These manufacturers were also interested in getting a piece of the expanding gentleman farmer market. Several International Harvester Company (IH) documents make note of the fact that in the midst of suburban expansion, the number of 5- to 20-acre farms was growing at a much higher rate than any other farm size in the country. Companies like IH, Allis-Chalmers, and several others scrambled to get products sized for these operations to market posthaste, and in some cases, they found themselves in competition with companies they had never heard of.

Farm Tractor Manufacturers Enter the Fray

It would be incorrect to suggest that only the tiny single-bottom plow tractors built by farm machinery manufacturers shortly after the war ever made it into the suburban garden or mowed suburban lawns. Many larger machines lived out their lives with such relatively light duty, but the few discussed in more detail in this chapter were particularly suited to working in larger gardens.

The Allis-Chalmers G made a better garden tractor than it did an estate machine. The G is still used by small food farmers all over the country, and many have been repowered with everything from Kubota diesel engines to battery packs and electric motors.

Allis-Chalmers Model G

The Model G, which was built from 1948 through 1955, might well be the most recognizable tractor out there. It was originally designed for small farms, nurseries, truck gardeners, and others with the need for a precision planting and cultivating machine. It also had excellent capabilities as an all-around acreage tractor. Early marketing materials suggested that the Model G and its implements at the most offered everything some farms required by way of machinery and at the least had something that every farm required.

What really set the G apart from other tractors of its day was that the engine was mounted behind the rear axle and the remaining tubular frame offered unprecedented visibility for the operator. The little tractor weighed in at around 1,200 pounds and offered about 9 drawbar horsepower and 10.33 horsepower at the PTO. Since Allis-Chalmers didn't make an engine small enough for the tractor, it sourced a four-cylinder 62-cubic-inch gasoline mill from Continental. This so-called N-62 engine was used by many machinery makers and proved itself again and again over the years.

Although the basic design never caught on in a big way, the Model G proved its worth and continues to be

International's Farmall Cub is one of the most highly collected farm tractors today. This 1952 model was refurbished in 2005 and hasn't seen a lick of work since.

collected, cherished, and worked today. In fact, the tractor is so good in the garden that at least one North American business is based on repowering the machines with small, efficient Kubota diesel engines and refurbishing their chassis for another 60-something years of work.

Modern garden tractor owners might scoff at the G's seemingly tiny horsepower ratings. After all, the major makers today all boast lawn tractors with over 20 horsepower. Of course, that rating is net engine horsepower, and only a fraction of it will be transferred to the ground with the 400-pound lawn cutter. If you hook your Allis-Chalmers Model G to a laden wagon, you will be able to move it long after the lawn tractor hooked to the same weight spins its wheels or, more likely, burns up its transmission.

The Farmall Cub is easy to haul and much less a handful than many other vintage tractors, so it is a favorite at plow days and other events around the country. Easy as it is to handle, the Cub was too expensive to be considered for general suburban use in the 1950s.

International Harvester Cub

Harvester's mighty little Cub was announced during a 1945 press event at the company's Hinsdale, Illinois, test farm. When it entered production in April 1947, the versatile little tractor was billed as the perfect machine for the small farmer and gentleman farmer and a chore boy for larger operators. The tractor featured IH's offset operator station, which was called Culti-Vision. Compared with the Allis-Chalmers Model G, this little workhorse looked like a fairly conventional row-crop tractor with the engine up front and transaxle to the rear.

The Cub was rated for a single-plow bottom and could be fit with any manner of cultivators, planters, mowers, grader blades, rakes, utility carriers, and much more. The tractor was powered with IH's four-cylinder C-60 60-cubic-inch gasoline engine and offered about 9.76 PTO horsepower initially, with almost 9 horsepower at the drawbar. As the machine evolved through its approximately three decades of production, its engine power increased to about 15 horsepower gross, which delivered about 13 horsepower at the PTO and 12 horsepower at the drawbar.

First known as the Farmall Cub, and later as the International Cub, some iteration of the Cub design played a direct role in IH's garden tractor lineup from 1961 through 1981. The initial design (with some changes over the years) was built from 1947 to 1978. The Cub in all of its forms continues to provide the power for gardens large and small all over the world. It is also one of the most desired collector tractors because

Although they were perfect for working on small farms and in gardens, John Deere's Models L and LA (shown here) were never terribly popular in suburban yards, in spite of their diminutive size.

it is easy to haul and easy to handle. As with the other tractors considered in this category, the 1,500- to 1,800-pound (depending on options) Cub had a drawbar pull of well over 1,200 pounds.

John Deere Model L

Although John Deere's Model L family of tractors fits the bill for this category with less than 10 horsepower at the drawbar and PTO and an approximate 1,500-pound mass, the machine was first built about a decade earlier than the Cub and its production ended in 1946, with no model replacement. First produced in about 1936 when Deere's Wagon Works built a tiny experimental eight-horsepower tractor called the Model Y, this tractor at first was powered with Novo two-cylinder engines. Folks seemed so pleased with these first 24 Model Y prototypes that Deere made 80 more the summer of 1937.

These tractors were powered with two-cylinder Hercules engines and given the Model 62 designation.

In late 1937, the Model 62 evolved into the Model L. This machine had very little sheet metal, which matched other Deere and Company offerings of the day. The first-generation Model L tractor was still powered with the two-cylinder Hercules and boasted a little more than 10 horsepower at the engine. In late 1938, the Model L got a facelift that included modern styling and eventually a 10-horsepower two-cylinder Deere and Company engine. The Model L was a fairly stripped-down machine that lacked hydraulics, but it could be fit with a number of lever-lifted attachments and pull- or push-type implements. It had about 7 drawbar horsepower, with 9.25 horsepower at the PTO.

In 1941, a slightly more powerful Model LA joined the Model L as a small Deere tractor. The LA offered

The Massey-Harris Pony was designed with the small farmer in mind and surely made its way to hundreds, if not thousands, of smaller vegetable or tobacco patches around the world. Though every bit as useful as the Farmall Cub and Allis-Chalmers G, the little Massey was never found very far from the farm.

a 540-rpm PTO, more ground clearance, and about 10.5 drawbar horsepower with almost 13 horsepower at the PTO. By the time both the L and LA were discontinued in 1946, the engine power in the LA was about that of the larger, more conventional-looking Model H. Deere and Company wouldn't re-enter the garden tractor niche again until the 1960s.

Massey-Harris Pony

Massey-Harris released the Pony 11 for the 1947 model year in a package that looked strikingly similar to the Farmall Cub, except that the tractor's driveline wasn't offset from the operator's station. The Pony came on the heels of the company's earlier offering in the small tractor arena, the General CG. Unwilling to commit to the small tractor market before the war, Massey-Harris had the General built by Cleveland Tractor Company. After the war, it was clear that the market for single-plow tractors was growing, so Massey introduced the Pony.

The Pony 11 was powered with Continental's N-62 four-cylinder gasoline engine and offered an 11-PTO horsepower rating, with 10 horsepower at the drawbar. The tractor tipped the scales at slightly over 1,500 pounds and could be equipped with hydraulics from the

In the early 1950s, Garden-All's Gard'n Mast'r could be equipped with all manner of attachments, including the belly-mounted sickle bar mower shown here.

beginning. The Pony 14 replaced the Pony 11 in 1950. It had a 69-cubic-inch version of the N-62 engine, which produced a couple of additional horsepower. The Pony 14 was replaced with the heavier, more powerful Pacer in 1954. This tractor was powered with Continental's Y-91 engine and bridged the gap between single- and two-plow tractors at the time. The Pacer was discontinued in 1956, and within about a decade, Massey had a line of modern garden tractors to offer the market.

Garden Tractor Manufacturers Hit Their Stride

Even though suburbanites and small-acreage owners were in the big tractor-makers' sights, these folks were being catered to by companies with a history of building yard-sized equipment and savvy entrepreneurs willing to work for a piece of the yet-to-be-defined market share. In postwar North America, a lot of energy was being poured into creating and selling four-wheel garden tractors.

In the 1948-1949 edition of Farm Implement News' *Tractor Field Book*, the machines now known as garden tractors were listed as tractors with less than a single

GIBSON MANUFACTURING AND THE MODEL D

Wilbur Gibson appears to have begun making garden tractors sometime before World War II (likely in the 1930s) in Seattle, but he produced relatively limited numbers throughout the years leading up to and during the war. By 1946, his company was called the Gibson Manufacturing Corporation and had moved to Longmont, Colorado—or at least that is where its corporate headquarters was listed. Tractors of that vintage often have both Seattle and Longmont cast into their rear-axle housings.

One of Gibson's most popular tractors was the Model D. In 1948, this machine was a lever-steered contraption that was both heavy and heavy-duty. It was powered with a 23-cubic-inch single-cylinder Wisconsin engine and could reportedly pull a 12-inch plow bottom through average soil. The tractor, like so many others of the day, lacked sheet metal of any kind. By 1951, the Model D had evolved into a very attractive and fully capable tractor with a nicely styled grille, hood, dash, and fenders. The Model D was still steered with a lever, and it featured detachable rear rims that could be mounted in any number of ways to vary the track width. The machine's shipping weight was listed as 1,020 pounds.

Just more than a year later, the Gibson Manufacturing Corporation was out of business, but it left a legacy of Model A, Model D, and Super D riding garden tractors and even a few Model H and Model I farm tractors. Gibson lore suggests that company records were burned when news of bankruptcy hit home and that Wilbur started another tractor company and then died shortly after Gibson Manufacturing closed its doors in the early 1950s.

This little Bantam is equipped with the shaft-driven 34-inch-width front-mount rotary mower. There was also a belly-mount mower available, along with a pair of sickle bar mowers.

Tiny as they are, members of the Bantam tractor lineup sported engines rated with three to eight horsepower, all-gear worm-drive differentials, and a collection of implements that included ground-engaging turning plows.

Billed as safe, educational, and fun, Strunk's Chipmunk shows the extremes that manufacturers were willing to go to for a piece of the suburban tractor market. This little machine was able to pull a cart, leaf sweeper, and either an 18 or 21-inch-cut reel mower. It was definitely not a garden tractor. *Author's collection*

BRADLEY: CATALOG-SOLD MACHINES

David Bradley is often credited with bringing the first pig iron to the city of Chicago, which he called home beginning in 1835. While in Chicago, he initially worked for Jones King & Company and helped build Chicago Furnace, the first foundry in the city. Bradley later took up farming in Lake County and eventually made bricks and agricultural machinery in nearby Racine, Wisconsin.

In 1854, after a stint in the lumber business in Michigan and at the age of 43, Bradley purchased a plow company from his brother-in-law and returned to Chicago. Later that year, he entered into a partnership with Conrad Furst to form Furst and Bradley, an agricultural implement manufacturing company with a line of wagons, plows, and cultivators.

By 1860, the partners had discontinued their wagon line to focus on more specialized implements. In need of development and operational capital, the partners incorporated in 1872 to form Furst & Bradley Manufacturing Company and sold stock in the business. By 1884, Furst was ready to retire, so Bradley and his son J. Harley Bradley bought Furst's shares and changed the company's name to the David Bradley Manufacturing Company.

The implement company moved from its location at Fulton and Des Plaines streets in Chicago to an old furniture factory near Kankakee, Illinois, in 1895. In 1910, Sears, Roebuck and Company purchased the company's assets (including the Kankakee plant, which was renamed the David Bradley Manufacturing Works) to round out its catalog's agricultural offerings. Interestingly, David Bradley's first tractor wasn't released until 1931. It was a two-wheeled model named the Handiman.

In 1938 Sears offered the full-sized Graham Bradley farm tractor through its catalog. It was the largest tractor ever built at the Bradley Works, and it was followed in 1939 by the manufacturing enterprise's first four-wheel riding garden tractor, which was dubbed the Handiman RT.

During World War II, the David Bradley Manufacturing Works was among the first to be converted to producing materiel, which included among other things engine parts and mortar shells. The plant earned the coveted Army-Navy E award

for its efforts. Shortly after the war, Sears replaced the Handiman garden tractor line with the David Bradley Garden Tractor. Several models of riding tractors came and went over the years. The company's unusual Tri-Trac model was introduced in 1954; the Suburban tractor lineup was released in 1959.

In 1962, Sears folded David Bradley into another company it owned, the Newark Ohio Company. In 1966, the George D. Roper Company purchased the Newark Ohio Company and continued to supply Sears with lawn and garden equipment for at least a decade. In 1983, Roper closed the Bradley Works in Kankakee. Most of the plant's remains were destroyed in a 1986 fire.

Roper, a pump specialist, sold off several of its nonessential businesses in the last two decades of the twentieth century, including the outdoor power products, which most recently became part of Electrolux's American Yard Products Company. American Yard Products builds parts and machines for names like Husqvarna, Poulan, Sears, Craftsman, and Roper, to name a few.

David Bradley's Handiman RT was marketed through Sears, Roebuck and Company's highly successful catalog in 1939. The machine was billed as a money-making partner that would pay for itself in no time. *Author's collection*

This 1957 Red-E Model 15 four-wheel garden tractor looks very much like many of the tractors that wore the Economy and Power King brands. Some garden tractor lore suggests that all three brands were related.

12-inch plow capacity. Machines that made the list included the Bolens Huski Ridemaster, Engineering Products Company's Economy, Gibson's Model D, Grand Haven Stamped Products Company's Model BC, Inexco Tractor Corporation's Tiger 12, Lincoln Tractor Company's Lincoln, Peco Manufacturing Corporation's Model TR47, Shaw Manufacturing Company's Model R7 and Model HY8, and Smathers Manufacturing Company's Acme Motor Cultivator. This is no doubt just a sampling of the companies that were in the business, but that they were in the book means they were interested in getting the word out about their machines.

By the time the 1951-1952 *Red Tractor Book* was published by *Implement and Tractor*, the number of manufacturers listed as producing light riding tractors had grown to well over twice that published in 1949. Familiar and not so familiar names that were added to the list included Beaver Riding Tractor, Gard'n Mast'r, Mayrath Mobile Tractor, Page (Pioneer Manufacturing Company), Power King (Power King Tractor Company), Roths BesRo (Roths Industries Inc.), and Waterbury Rider.

For the most part, these riding garden tractors had four wheels, multiple speeds, and engines up front. The Page and Grand Haven BC had the engine in back and looked quite a bit like small versions of the Allis-Chalmers

This is the Red-E tractor's grille and decal.

Model G. These machines used everything from belt- or chain-drive systems to automotive-style transmissions and rear axles. Some machines used belt-idler-style clutches, while others used the heavier-duty single-disc friction clutches found on most light trucks and larger tractors of the day. The following companies provided the machines' engines: Wisconsin, Briggs & Stratton, Clinton, Salsbury, Kohler, and others. Most of the tractors could pull an eight-inch plow through the soil, and they weighed anywhere from about 500 pounds to more than 1,600 pounds. In any case, they weighed enough to transmit the bulk of their meager four to eight horsepower to the ground, and most could still out-pull modern-day versions.

A beautifully restored 1957 Bolens Ride-A-Matic Deluxe. Note the heavy cast nose piece, an important component to keeping the machine balanced with rear attachments mounted.

Bolens

It was 1947 when the Bolens Huski Ridemaster four-wheel garden tractor came on the scene. The machine looked for all intents and purposes like a two-wheeled garden tractor grafted to a more purpose-built sulky than most other sulkies of the day. The articulated Ridemaster was steered with a wheel connected to the vehicle's pivot point. By turning the wheel, the entire front drive bogey turned. The operator was perched on the rear bogey that consisted of a trailing frame with attachment points for cultivators and other implements. Food Machinery Corporation (FMC) marketed the Ridemaster with a Wisconsin engine as the Bean Cutler Tractor for use in California's vineyards at the same time the Bolens-

A close-up of the Bolens Ride-A-Matic heavy grille casting and decal. Note the reference to Food Machinery Corporation on the decal.

branded version was released. The Huski Ridemaster was offered through the late 1940s to 1958 with various Wisconsin and Briggs & Stratton engines in the six- to

This 1954 Bolens Ride-A-Matic sports a custom-colored paint job to the delight of its owner. Note that even at this early age, the Bolens tractor could be equipped with electric starting.

eight-horsepower range. By the time it was discontinued, attachments such as cultivators, mowers, blades, land plows, and more were available.

By 1957, the market demanded more user-friendly, automotive-like machines. Bolens delivered with the Ride-A-Matic 20HD. This heavy-duty four-wheel garden tractor was powered with a four-horsepower Kohler engine. It was also available as the 21HD with Kohler's seven-horsepower engine. The Ride-A-Matic shared many components with the two-wheeled Versa-Matic and was fully capable of pulling ground-engaging tools. It weighed well over 500 pounds, a lot lighter than Ridemaster's 925-pound mass. In 1958, the Ride-A-Matic 21HD was renamed the Model 220, while the 20HD became the 200. The remaining Ridemaster variants

were renamed as Models 112 and 113. This was the last year for the Ridemaster.

In 1959, a single manual-start Ride-A-Matic Model 230 was listed as a company offering.

David Bradley

By 1939, Sears was selling David Bradley's Handiman RT, a little tractor that looked like a full-fledged farm tractor. It was powered with a Briggs & Stratton Model Z engine that transmitted power to the rear wheels through a belt-idler clutch, two-speed transmission, and single-gear reduction differential. The little four-wheeled machine also had independent rear brakes. The Handiman RT appears to have been marketed for several years, but it was the walking tractors that kept Sears in the market for decades.

David Bradley's Handiman RT riding tractor was built for Sears as a complement to the walking Handiman tractor lineup in the late 1930s. The name was eventually changed to Suburban to avoid confusing Sears's riding and walking tractor lines.

In the early 1950s, at the behest of Sears, David Bradley engineers went to work on an entirely new concept in riding garden tractors. The machine, known as the Tri-Trac, was actually born in Sears' own engineering department and was designed to solve expensive manufacturing issues; however, it wound up creating more and ultimately was nothing short of a disaster. According to David Bradley lore, Sears engineers felt that one significant problem with developing inexpensive garden tractors was the complexity of the final drive system, most notably the differential. Their idea was to create a

garden tractor without a differential, which would so reduce manufacturing costs that Sears might make some headway in the riding garden tractor market, which its earlier products had not managed to do.

Sears engineers responded with a novel tricycle design that put a single drive wheel in back and a pair of steering wheels up front. The operator straddled the machine as one might straddle a motorcycle. The Tri-Trac not only looked goofy, but it behaved poorly too. The Tri-Trac was released in 1954 and wound up being expensive, cumbersome, and unstable. The roughly 600-pound

PANZER: THE PENNSYLVANIA CONNECTION

The story behind Panzer tractors begins in the early 1950s with an engineer named Jim Clark, who was frustrated by the clumsiness of a two-wheeled walking tractor he rented to help landscape his new home in the Washington, D.C., suburb of College Park, Maryland. Jim felt there had to be a better way to do this type of work, so he interviewed market gardeners, farmers, and university personnel and came up with a prototype machine in 1953. Company lore indicates that this first attempt was nothing short of a disaster, but it led directly to a redesign that included a narrowed Dodge rear axle with individual steering brakes and a belt-idler-type clutch.

Jim was working at Ahrendt Instrument Company (a leading manufacturer of precision instrumentation and a servomechanism innovator) at the time, and his boss took an interest in the tractor, suggesting that they form a company to produce it. The company was born in 1954 as COPAR Manufacturing, and the first several hundred Panzer three-wheeled tractors came off the line. According to Panzer historians, the machine got its moniker by way of a naming contest.

COPAR's success with the little garden tractors was significant enough that production quickly needed to be moved out of the Ahrendt facility. The company moved to a renovated plant in Laurel, Maryland, in 1955 and stayed there until 1960. Several models of three-wheel and four-wheel garden tractors were produced there—about 10,000 total by most accounts.

In 1960, COPAR was sold to Virginia Metalcrafters (VM) of Waynesboro, and within a year of ownership, VM had tightened up the line by discontinuing the larger three- and four-wheeled models and concentrating on the so-called light tractor line. The Panzer brand gained popularity, loyalty, and utility under VM's ownership. In an interesting twist, VM purchased Pennsylvania Lawnmowers, a venerable mower manufacturer, in 1963. By 1964, Panzers were sold as products of the Pennsylvania Lawn Products Company, and just a couple of years later the tractors were marketed as the Pennsylvania Panzer.

Schenuit Industries, Inc., of Baltimore, Maryland, purchased Pennsylvania Lawn Products in 1970 and combined it with Jackson Manufacturing Company, a garden-tool maker Schenuit already owned. Panzer's immediate parent was renamed the Pennsylvania Lawn Products Division of Jackson Manufacturing, and all production was moved to Martinsburg, West Virginia. By the end of the year, the Panzer line was completely discontinued.

Schenuit went into receivership in 1971, and Jackson was sold off as part of the settlement. Dandy Sales, Inc., wound up with the patterns and prints for all of the Pennsylvania Panzers, and it continues to supply parts for the tractors to this day.

The Panzer was a well-built and heavy-duty tractor. Note the heavy cast grille and the offset driveshaft that is powered from the front of the engine.

SIMPLICITY: THE LAUNCH OF
THE WONDERBOY 700

Tractor maker Simplicity owes its name to a turn-of-the-twentieth-century gasoline engine built and marketed by Western Malleable and Gray Iron Manufacturing Company of Milwaukee, Wisconsin. That company was formed in 1872, but didn't offer the Simplicity engine until several decades later. In 1911, Western was taken over by L. M. Turner, who renamed it Turner Manufacturing and moved the company to Port Washington, Wisconsin. Turner Manufacturing continued to produce engines and farm tractors at that location until shortly after World War I.

In 1920, Turner was liquidated, with the Simplicity name and some other company assets going to William Niederkorn, Turner's former sales manager. Niederkorn formed the Simplicity Manufacturing Company in 1922 and began producing machines and tools for the automotive industry—including a cylinder-boring machine used to rebuild engines. As part of a diversification plan, Simplicity went after the garden equipment market in 1937 with a two-wheeled tractor marketed exclusively through the catalog giant Montgomery Ward and Company.

The Simplicity machines sold well, and the company's first rider, sold in 1939, was really a walk-behind model equipped with a sulky. Simplicity offered a true riding mower, called the Wonderboy, in the early 1950s. The company's first four-wheel garden tractor, known as the Wonderboy 700, was released in 1959. Throughout the rest of the twentieth century, the company produced a full line of lawn and garden equipment, including true garden tractors.

During the early 1960s, Simplicity was also producing garden tractors for Allis-Chalmers. The well-established farm-equipment manufacturer purchased Simplicity in 1965 and continued manufacturing at Simplicity's Port Washington location. Federal fair-trade laws forced Allis-Chalmers to open another plant to build its garden tractors, this one in Lexington, South Carolina. Once the fair-trade laws were repealed in the mid-1970s, Allis closed the Lexington plant, and all garden tractor manufacturing was moved back to the Simplicity plant in Port Washington.

Allis-Chalmers sold its agricultural businesses to Deutz in 1984, but Simplicity was not included in the deal. Simplicity continued to produce garden tractors under the Deutz-Allis name, however, until AGCO was formed to purchase the remains of Deutz-Allis in 1991. At that point, the tractor color changed back to orange from Deutz's lime green.

Allis-Chalmers spun Simplicity off in 1983 to some members of management and an investment group known as the Westray Corporation. In 1985, the Employee Stock Owners Trust (ESOT) group formed to buy Simplicity back from Westray, which made company employees the principal owners. In 1994, ESOT sold a majority of its holding in Simplicity to a private investment firm.

In 1999, Simplicity acquired Ferris Industries, a maker of professional turf-care equipment. Snapper then joined Ferris in the Simplicity fold in 2002. In 2004, Briggs & Stratton's Power Products Group purchased Simplicity, and the brand lives on.

It's interesting to note that over the years Simplicity Manufacturing built garden tractors under its own brand and those of Allis-Chalmers, Montgomery Ward, J. C. Penney, Homelite, Massey Ferguson, AGCO-Allis, AGCO, Deutz-Allis, and several Canadian groups such as Eaton.

tractor (with no operator or attachments) wasn't terribly robust with its six-horsepower engine and didn't last long in the Sears catalog.

In 1959, Sears released its excellent Suburban line of riding garden tractors, and they served gardeners and the company well for many years.

Engineering Products Company

This company began building small garden tractors in Milwaukee, Wisconsin, in about 1946. At least some production moved to Waukesha in the late 1940s or early 1950s and later moved again to Beaver Dam. The company's initial four-wheel tractor offering was the Economy, powered with a Wisconsin or Briggs & Stratton engine.

The David-Bradley Tri-Trac was designed by Sears engineers to be an economical, easy-to-maintain alternative to the other garden tractors of the day. In the end, it was a spectacular flop that proved to be underpowered, overweight, and unstable.

The 700-plus-pound machine produced around six horsepower and could pull a single 10-inch plow. The tractor was formed with a steel channel frame that positioned the engine between the front bolster and rear axle. The engine's power was fed to the rear wheels through a single-disc dry clutch (produced by Rockford), three-speed transmission (produced by BorgWarner), differential (produced by BorgWarner), and shortened rear axle. The differential shaft ends were fit with bull-pinion gears that engaged larger bull gears in drop-box-style final drives. The bull gears were directly mounted to the left and right rear-axle shafts. The operator could steer with a steering wheel that in early years was coupled to a chain system and later to a Ross automotive-type gear.

The Economy was a heavy-duty machine with plenty of pull for most gardens. It could also be fit with a belly-mount sickle bar mower in addition to a plow, cultivators, planters, and the like. The tractor lacked sheet metal of any kind other than the cooling shroud on the engine and looked very much like the unstyled farm tractors so prevalent before World War II.

During the Economy's early tenure, another manufacturer, Power King Tractor Company of Milwaukee, offered a tiller-steered tractor that looked very similar to the Economy and indeed also used some of the same Crosley components in the drivetrain. Economy Power King lore suggests that this company was part of the Engineering Products Company, but that cannot be confirmed. What is clear is that in the 1952

Shaw: Success Comes at Early Age

Stanley Shaw showed an incredible mechanical aptitude at a very early age. By the time he was nine years old, he had built a functional person-powered machine from bits and pieces he found in a junk pile and called it a tractor. Young Stanley steered the device with his knees and powered it with a hand crank. In 1895, when he was barely 14 years old, he is said to have built a small steam engine by using commonly available pump parts, and by 1902 he had constructed a crude, but operable gasoline engine.

Shaw opened his Shaw Manufacturing Company in Galesburg, Kansas, in 1903, at the age of 22. Among other things, he built and sold engines and the Shawmobile auto from that location. In 1911, he purchased the Kokomo Bicycle Company of Kokomo, Indiana. At first, he planned to move his growing manufacturing company to that location, but he later was convinced to stay in Galesburg, where his family built him a new factory.

Shaw entered the tractor business in the early 1920s with at least two walking models and Ford Model T car conversions. In 1938, the company offered its first four-wheel riding tractor, the Model RD. This machine was based on the Model D and included a sulky-like attachment (with rear-wheel steer as opposed to articulation) and a deluxe engine hood. This tractor series eventually gave way to the more conventionally oriented riding garden tractors, initially fitted with Ford drivetrain components.

Stanley Shaw continued to operate his manufacturing company from Galesburg until 1962, when he sold it to Bush Hog. He was 81 years old at the time.

and later *Implement and Tractor* magazines and *Red Tractor Books*, both Power King and Engineering Products Company models are listed, and Power King tractors are advertised as being produced by Engineering Products Company.

In 1951, the Power King could be fitted with either Briggs & Stratton or Wisconsin power and offered hydraulics as an option. The tractor was tiller steered, used chain reduction in the final drives, and weighed only 750 pounds. Like the early Economy, this tractor was also unstyled.

Through the 1950s, Engineering Products Company offered tractors wearing both the Economy Power King and the Economy brands. Models included wheel-steered and tiller-steered units with names like Economy Special, Estate, Country Squire, Power Queen, and Jim Dandy, which was a smaller-framed unit that appeared in late January of 1957. Most of these tractors were powered with a choice of Briggs & Stratton or Wisconsin engines and looked a little more refined because the engine sheet metal offered a grille-like look to the front end; a small hood sheet and dash were also part of the package. By the end of the decade, at least three different models were available.

COPAR and Panzer

Panzer garden tractors were first available in 1954 and included the 580-pound Model A (later the Model T102). The tractor, powered by a nine-horsepower Briggs & Stratton engine in 1955, looked like a tricycle-style row-crop farm tractor and was equipped with a single wheel up front. With three forward gears and 16-inch lugged rear tires, the little machine could pull. In 1956, it was available with an implement lift, plow, seeder, cultivators, mowers, and many other attachments.

In 1958, the T102 was replaced with the four-wheeled T205. These so-called large Panzer models were joined or replaced by several others—the T110, T205, T210, T115, T120, T215, and T220—through 1960, as well as smaller models such as the T50, T55, T60, and T65.

Although this is a 1960 model, this unstyled Economy tractor is typical of the Economy and Power King models that preceded it. Note that the steering wheel is attached to an offset Ross automotive-style steering gear.

Simplicity

Although Simplicity played an important role in the walking tractor market directly after World War II, it didn't offer a true riding garden tractor, the Wonderboy 700, until 1959. This tractor had a seven-horsepower Briggs & Stratton engine that fed power to the transaxle through a shaft coupled to the flywheel and belt-idler clutch system located aft. The tractor had three forward speeds, delivered through a combination of sliding spiral bevel gears and spur gear transmission. The Wonderboy 700 tipped the scales at over 500 pounds and could be equipped with many attachments, including cultivators, a land plow, a grader blade, a snow thrower, a disc, rotary tiller, mowers, and many other tools. The Wonderboy 700's name was changed

to the 700 for 1960 to avoid confusion with the company's Wonderboy line of walking tractors.

Speedex

After World War II, in about 1949, Harold Pond's Speedex brand resurfaced in full force. His Ford-based Models B and FG had done fairly well beforehand and continued to immediately after the war. By the end of the 1940s, however, Pond was well on his way to developing a transmission and drive axle of his own because old Ford parts were more difficult to source.

In 1950, Pond released his tiller-steered Model 23 that sported the new drivetrain. The Model 23 was powered with an eight-horsepower Briggs & Stratton engine,

WHEEL HORSE: A FATHER-SON OPERATION

Wheel Horse corporate lore has it that Elmer Pond and his son Cecil formed their Pond Tractor Company in 1946 after many years of assembling, improving on, and selling Speedex tractors for Elmer's brother Harold. By then, the father-son team had discovered it unlikely that Speedex assembly and sales could support two households, so Cecil is said to have suggested that he and his father make their own tractors, particularly since the fit and finish on Harold's wasn't terribly good.

The enterprise borrowed heavily from the Speedex model, creating machines from readily available bits and pieces, but Elmer and Cecil were committed to making parts more accurately to avoid assembly headaches. In 1947, they released the first garden tractor, simply called the Pond Tractor. Not surprisingly, the Pond Tractor was an open-framed, lever-steered contraption that resembled Harold's Speedex machines more than a little. In the early years, Elmer and Cecil sourced drivetrains for the tractors from junkyards, but they made their own pinion and bull-gear-style final drives, much like those found on Farmall tractors of the day.

Although they had worked together for years, it wasn't until the first day of 1948 that the father and son team formalized their partnership. That same year, a two-wheeled tractor design joined their four-wheel model. By 1956, the phrase "Wheel Horse" had been used by the pair to describe some of their machines. That very year, the Pond Tractor Company was renamed Wheel Horse Products Company. Wheel Horse expanded its lineup and gained market share over the next several years and today remains one of the most respected names in garden tractors.

In 1974, Wheel Horse Products was merged into American Motors Corporation's (AMC) wholly owned subsidiary Wheel Horse Delaware, which was created specifically for the acquisition. AMC had no big changes in mind initially, so the tractor lineup didn't change much. That same year, Wheel Horse electric models were made available since the company had negotiated the purchase of General Electric's Elec-Trak tractors before the merger.

In 1982, the Munn Investment Group bought Wheel Horse, and in 1986 Toro acquired the brand. Garden tractors with the Wheel Horse brand on them and many vintage parts are still available through Toro.

Wheel Horse released the Ride-Away Junior in the late 1950s. From very early on, it was equipped with the company's proprietary transaxle and could be fit with all manner of implements, such as the front-mounted sickle bar mower and rear-mounted land plow shown here.

sold for $350, and featured right-hand tiller steering control. Other models, such as the Clinton-powered D4 and M Series tractors, followed the Model 23. All of these tractors could be equipped with a full line of tools for farm, garden, and lawn chores.

The M Series tractors appear to have been accompanied by, or in some cases replaced by, the S-14 and S-23 right around 1959. Both the S-14 and S-23 used a sliding engine belt-tightening clutch system. The S-14 was initially powered with a 5.75-horsepower Briggs

The Wheel Horse Ride-Away Senior used surplus Ford parts and could be ordered with or without the fiberglass hood, which is shown here. Rumor has it that the Ponds made the hoods to order by hand.

& Stratton engine that was replaced by a 6-horsepower model later. The S-23 featured a 9-horsepower Briggs & Stratton powerplant. The shipping weights·on the S-14 and S-23 were 365 pounds and 700 pounds, respectively. The smaller machine was rated for a single 8-inch plow and offered a steering wheel, while the S-23 could handle a 10-inch bottom plow and still employed the lever or tiller steering system. These were the only two Speedex tractors to make the 1962 *Implement and Tractor Red Tractor Book*, and by then both offered a steering wheel.

Shaw Manufacturing

Shaw's nicely styled R Series Du-All riding garden tractors came on line in 1945. By 1947, the offerings included the Model R7 and HY8 (high clearance model). The nearly 1,300-pound four-wheel R7 was powered with a 7.75-horsepower Briggs & Stratton engine and was rated to pull a 10-inch land plow. The 9-horsepower Wisconsin-powered HY8 tipped the scales at nearly 1,400 pounds and was reported to be able to handle a 12-inch plow. Both tractors had three-speed gear sets and featured Rockwell dry-disc clutches. The Shaw tractors really bridged the gap between true garden tractors and small farm tractors.

By 1956, Shaw's riding garden tractor models included the N8 and R8. Both were equipped with four wheels, but they were about half the mass of their predecessors. The N8 weighed 780 pounds, while the R8 came in at about 950 pounds. Both tractors could be equipped

The right side view of the Ride-Away Senior clearly shows the heavy-duty automotive transmission and rear axle. This model was discontinued in 1956.

with Briggs & Stratton or Wisconsin engines in the seven-to nine-horsepower range. This new pair of Du-Alls featured three-speed sliding spur-gear transmissions, Ross cam and lever steering gears, and independent rear brakes. The N8 used shoes and the R8 had band brakes. Stout components like Rockford dry-disc clutches and robust drop-box-style final drives made these tractors real workhorses. Both machines were available into the late 1950s.

Wheel Horse

In 1946, Cecil and Elmer Pond broke away from building tractors for Elmer's brother Harold and struck out on their own. The first four-wheel garden tractor the father-son duo came up with was simply called the Pond

Tractor. This machine had an overall structure and design that was quite similar to Harold's right-hand tiller-steered machines of the day.

The little machine was powered with a six-horsepower Briggs & Stratton engine that was securely fixed in the angle-iron frame. Power from the engine fed to the Ford Model A transmission through a BorgWarner single-disc, dry, over-center-type clutch. Transmission output routed through a driveshaft fabricated by the father-and-son team to the Ford Model T differential. The final drives consisted of drop-box-style bull and bull-pinion gear arrangements. These parts were also fabricated for the machine. Steering was by way of a lever.

In 1948, when Ford Model A transmissions were getting scarce, many Pond tractors were equipped with

The Page garden tractor was very much a knockoff of the Allis-Chalmers Model G, although it was quite a bit smaller. This is a beautifully restored 1951 model.

a Ford V-8 transmission. Briggs & Stratton didn't approve its engines for use with the spring-loaded clutch that went with that transmission, so the tractors were equipped with 8.33-horsepower Wisconsins. At the same time, a Ross steering gear was substituted for the lever, and a steering wheel was put in place. This tractor was manufactured with some tweaks, changes, and improvements for several years. In 1955, it was named the RS-83 Ride-Away Senior and could be ordered with or without a fiberglass hood.

The RJ-25 and RJ-35 Ride-Away Junior models were released that same year. The eight-inch-plow-capacity Ride-Away Junior tractors had five-speed transmissions and 2.5-horsepower Briggs & Stratton powerplants on the RJ-25s or 3.6-horsepower Clinton or Kohler engines on the RJ-35s. Power transmission was via belt idlers and variable-pitch pulleys. These tractors were styled with a one-piece hood and solid grille.

The Ride-Away Senior was discontinued in 1956, which is the same year the company was officially renamed Wheel Horse. The RJ-25 was discontinued that same year. In 1958, the RJ-35 was replaced with the RJ-58, and in 1959, it became the RJ-59. These machines used a 3.6-horsepower Clinton engine or 4-horsepower Kohler engine and no longer used the complicated belt transmission of the early Ride-Away Juniors. They used a three-speed Wheel Horse–designed transaxle system called the Uni-Drive.

All the Pond and Wheel Horse tractors could be equipped with any manner of garden and lawn implements. At slightly over 300 pounds, the Ride-Away Junior machines were light in the garden tractor class, but they served the market well.

This 1961 Cub Cadet model is in original condition and is still on the job in southcentral Pennsylvania. Note the early 38-inch deck with timing-belt drive.

CHAPTER
3

GETTING DOWN TO
BUSINESS (1960–1969)

The United States had survived its first postwar recession, the American Dream was thriving, people were moving to the suburbs in droves, and the number of small farms located close to urban areas was still growing by the late 1950s. The urban exodus wasn't just a short-lived postwar phenomenon; it was a fact of life that put huge demands on the lawn and garden equipment industry, which really haven't let up since.

In the 1960s, the incredible expansion in the garden tractor market continued, making it nearly impossible to cover all the manufacturers putting out models at the time in this chapter. This is the decade when many farm-equipment manufacturers finally realized that they were missing the boat by not serving the suburban public. Some of these companies built their own machines from scratch, while others contracted with established makers to speed their brand to market.

Allis-Chalmers

Allis-Chalmers' Model G was already five years out of production, so the company entered the 1960s without much of a presence at all in suburbia, but that was about to change. Allis-Chalmers' approach to the new market was to contract with Simplicity for a single model in 1961.

The partnership made sense, since Simplicity was only 40 miles away and had established itself as a quality player in the garden tractor arena. In 1962, Allis-Chalmers' first year in the suburban garden tractor market, the company offered Simplicity's seven-horsepower model as the Allis-Chalmers B-1 garden tractor.

The B-1 was powered with a 7.25-horsepower Briggs & Stratton engine, had a three-speed transmission (plus reverse), and offered electric start and front remote hydraulics as standard equipment. Unlike Allis-Chalmers' large tractors of the day, the B-1 was not painted orange; its colors were more reminiscent of the company's yellow-colored industrial line. The B-1 could be fitted with many attachments, including a belly mower, a sickle-bar mower, a reel-type gang mower, a cultivator, a seeder, a land plow, grader blades, and much more.

By 1963, customers were demanding more power, and the B-1 was replaced with the nine-horsepower Briggs & Stratton–powered B-10. That machine was actually rated at 10 horsepower and in 1965 was called the Big Ten. In late 1966, the 12-horsepower B-12 came on the scene. The B-10 and B-12 tractors shared a chassis, and by this time, they both had optional electric start on the entry-level models.

The Allis-Chalmers B-10 replaced the B-1 and was also built by Simplicity. The tractor was billed as an all-season workhorse. *Author's collection*

Allis-Chalmers purchased Simplicity in 1965, but it was operated as a wholly owned subsidiary and kept the same name. In 1968, Allis-Chalmers opened a plant in Lexington, South Carolina, to assuage federal government antitrust concerns. The first tractors out of that plant included the Models B-207, B-110, and B-112. These tractors were all similar to their predecessors, although the B-207 was lighter duty and used a vertical-shaft engine. Simplicity-branded garden tractors continued to be produced at the Port Washington plant.

By the end of the decade, Simplicity engineers had new transmissions, including hydrostatics and other modern features, in the works for the company's new garden tractor models.

International Harvester Cub Cadet

The Cub Cadet story begins in the late 1950s, when IH's farm equipment product planning group first documented its interest in the developing market for small, single-cylinder, air-cooled-engine-powered, four-wheeled tractors in the four- to seven- horsepower range. IH corporate memos document that the key players in the garden tractor market in 1958 and 1959 were Bolens, Wheel Horse, and Simplicity. Wheel Horse had an estimated

Standard equipment on the Allis-Chalmers B-10 included a 12-volt electric starter/generator, push-button starting, controlled-traction differential, and three PTO centers (front, middle, and rear). *Author's collection*

You'll like the extra leisure the B-10 gives you for really enjoying your lawn and garden. The complete set of attachments, easy fingertip controls and fast hookup make B-10 gardening fun. The B-10 is a quality-built tractor from the folks who make the big ones.

10,000 unit sales in 1958, so Harvester's sales group estimated that in 1960 or 1961 it could sell at least 5,000 tractors in the same category. History has proven that that estimate was well off the mark, as more than 49,000 Cub Cadet garden tractors were delivered in the first two years of production.

Before IH developed the Cub Cadet, the company considered including two garden tractors made by Wagner Iron Works of Milwaukee in its line. Wagner had been supplying loader and backhoe attachments for Harvester's line of industrial and utility tractors. Wagner's garden tractor was called the Little Giant, even though the company evidently supplied a single unit named Big Giant to International Harvester's engineering department for testing.

According to IH memos, the Wagner Big Giant "did not conform to the standard required in a product bearing the IH insignia." Corporate Tractor Committee Report 26 formally rejected the Wagner inclusion.

By the time the Big Giant had been excluded as an option for Harvester's entry into the garden tractor market, the company had initiated the rapid development of a corporate machine that would establish IH as a premier maker of lawn and garden equipment. The proposed tractor was without a firm name for much of its development. Cub-Ette, Cubette, Cub-Urban, and Ranch-All were considered early. By 1960, the tractor was born on paper, and its design included a seven-horsepower Kohler engine, a Farmall Cub three-speed transmission and differential, and cam and follower automotive-type

Although the Big Giant from Wagner Iron Works was likely never painted with these International Harvester Colors, this Little Giant model shows the clear resemblance of the line to IH's farm tractors of the day. The Wagner was never given serious consideration as IH's garden tractor, but it played a role in its development.

An engineering mockup of one IH garden tractor concept called the Cubette. The hood, grille, and transaxle were all borrowed directly from the Farmall Cub. *Author's collection*

steering. The target price of $512 was on the high end of the perceived competition.

In January 1961, after several mockups, and experimental, prototype, and preproduction machines had been built and tested, the Cub Cadet entered regular production at Harvester's Louisville plant. By 1963, at the end of the first-generation Cub Cadet's production run, about 63,000 units had been sold.

In late 1963, restyled and slightly redesigned Cub Cadet Models 70 and 100 were released to replace what is now referred to as the Cub Cadet Original. The Model 70 used a 7-horsepower Kohler, while the Model 100 had a 10-horsepower engine built by the same manufacturer. Both tractors continued to use the Cub's transaxle, and both used a single-disc dry clutch.

In 1965, the Model 70 was replaced with a freshly styled Model 71, the 100 was replaced with the 102, and a third 12-horsepower Model 122 came on line. These tractors were slightly more sophisticated in their styling and their design, but many chassis parts still overlapped

with earlier iterations. In the fall of 1965, IH added the Model 123 to its line. This 12-horsepower tractor was the first with a hydrostatic drive, a Sunstrand Company Model 15-U hydrostatic transmission coupled to the Cub's differential through a reduction gear. The cast-iron transmission case served as the hydraulic fluid reservoir. The design, an innovation of Sunstrand engineer Charles Ricketts, was a hard sell to IH.

Ricketts began work on the small hydrostatic transmission design in the early 1960s, and by 1963 he had fitted two Cub Cadet Originals with prototype transmissions for testing. Within seconds of his first prototype's trial run, he flipped it over backwards. In that first design, the speed/direction control lever was connected directly to the pump's swash plate, which made feathering virtually impossible. Shortly after that trial, Ricketts had a lever and cam interface between the speed/direction control lever and the swash plate, which greatly improved the tractor's performance.

International Harvester marketed the hydrostatic Cub Cadet Model 123 at county fairs around the country through a circus show of sorts that was designed to show off the new tractor's maneuverability, agility, and direc-

This Cubette was fabricated by Cub Cadet enthusiast Tim Delooza by using photographs and interviews with engineers who worked on the Cub Cadet project at the beginning. Note that the Cubette used the full-sized pan seat of larger farm tractors.

tional changeability. According to an article in *Harvester World*, more than 350,000 folks watched the show in western states alone. The straight man for the act was an unlikely animal trainer named Fearless Frisbee. He used whips and a pistol to keep several Model 123s in line and doing tricks. In this case, though, the tractors were painted with tiger stripes or leopard spots, and each also had a face, ears, and tail. Highly skilled operators pulled wheelies, causing their tractors to rear up at Fearless Frisbee. In other antics, operators jumped their wild-cat tractors over ramps, took corners on two wheels, and changed direction so rapidly that they sent gravel into the air and Fearless Frisbee heading for cover—much to the crowd's delight. The marketing show was no doubt a success, although no one could have known then that the entire Cub Cadet line would be hydrostatically driven in the future.

IH's second engineering mockup called the Cub-Ette used a new front casting and the Farmall Cub's fuel-tank skin as a hood. This tractor was painted red and white. *Author's collection*

This Cub Cadet prototype (one of ten reportedly built) looks quite a bit like the production machine, but there are many subtle differences, including one-of-a-kind castings and fenders.

In 1967, a revised and expanded Cub Cadet lineup was released with new styling and a quick-attach front implement carrier. The Models 72 and 104 replaced the Models 71 and 102. A new 10-horsepower hydrostatic Model 105 was added. The Model 124 replaced the 122, and the 125 hydro replaced the 123. In two years' time, these machines were replaced with the updated 73, 106, 107 (hydro), 126, and 127 (hydro). One of the most notable differences with these tractors is in their one-piece stamped-steel seat platform and fenders. In November 1969, a 14-horsepower Model 147 was added to the line. This high-end tractor had an electric lift and modified frame (notched to fit the bigger blower housing of the 14-horsepower Kohler), in addition to other enhancements that ultimately marked the end of the line for Cub Cadets based on the second-generation frame.

John Deere

In the late 1950s, Deere and Company was working through a massive redesign in its farm tractor lineup. The change involved moving from transversely mounted two-cylinder engines to longitudinally mounted multiple-cylinder units. The change was significant and would have a huge impact on the company's reputation and bottom line. In retrospect, it wasn't surprising that management rebuffed the Horicon, Wisconsin, plant engineers' attempts to get a corporate garden tractor going in 1959.

Not satisfied to take no for a final answer, Deere and Company's Horicon, Wisconsin, plant personnel kept the pressure on and even went so far as to point out the successes International Harvester was having with its Cub Cadet. Additional pressure came from engi-

This Kitty Kat has been restored to look like one of the promotional Model 123 Hydro Cub Cadets that IH used in its circus show. This tractor featured a 12-horsepower Kohler engine and a Sunstrand hydro. Speed and direction were controlled with a single lever on the dash.

The third-generation 12-horsepower gear-driven Cub Cadet was called the 122. Note the barbeque-style grille. This beautifully restored machine even has the original-style padded seat with fiberglass pan.

Believe it or not, this early Model 110 John Deere gets routine use at garden tractor plow day and pulling events.

neering, manufacturing, sales, and even dealers around the country, who in many cases had picked up other garden tractor contracts to round out their offerings. In a rare moment of reversal, Deere management changed its stance on the garden tractor question in the early 1960s and gave a cautious go ahead with the goal of getting a garden tractor to production by midyear in 1963.

Engineers involved with the Model L, LI, and LA were transferred to Horicon in support of the project in late 1962. By August 1963, 1,000 Model 110 garden tractors had rolled out the door and into the hands of a few select branches and dealers. The little green machine was powered with a seven-horsepower, single-cylinder Kohler, and it featured a belt-idler clutch and three-forward-speed transaxle. Ground speed in any gear could be varied with the help of a lever and pulley system located between the engine and transaxle.

Even though the sales season was for the most part over when the first 1,000 Model 110s came under the public's scrutiny, they were instantly loved. So by November 1963, Deere and Company management approved a resumption of the 110's production.

The Model 110 received Kohler's eight-horsepower engine in 1964 and a four-speed creeper transmission in time for the 1965 model year. Some styling improvements were made in that timeframe also; for example, the fiberglass fenders were replaced with larger stamped-steel versions. The hydraulic lift was introduced in late 1964 for the 1965 model year, and tractors so equipped are designated the Model 110H.

Just as with every other area in motorized agriculture, virtually all constituents still wanted more power in their John Deere garden tractor, so Deere released the 12-horsepower Model 112 and 112H in the summer of

Deere and Company's Model 112 could be equipped with an electric lift, which made raising heavy implements like land plows very easy. This restored machine is still on the job in central Pennsylvania.

The so-called patio 110 garden tractors didn't do well at the time, but they are incredibly valuable today as collector items. Note the later fender style on this late 1960s Spruce Blue version.

1966. These machines were effectively identical to the 110 and 110H except for the engine, which was a 10-horsepower Tecumseh.

Styling changes in the 110 and 112 lines included a one-piece stamped-steel fender/seat pedestal/operator platform, which replaced several individual pieces that were bolted together in earlier iterations.

In 1968, Deere and Company embarked on a marketing campaign that let owners choose a tractor with colors to match their individual sensibilities. The chassis on these tractors was painted Dogwood White, while the hoods and seats were available in colors like Patio Red, April Yellow, Spruce Blue, and Sunset Orange. Of course, the traditional John Deere Green and Highway Yellow version was also available. Sadly, this color extravaganza caused quite a bit of consternation among buyers

Deere's Model 140 was billed as much more tractor than it actually was, but it is a capable machine and has proved very popular at plowing events with its well-engineered hydraulics, steering brakes, and hydrostatic transmission.

and gave parts personnel an expensive headache. By the early 1970s, the custom color option was discontinued.

In 1968, Deere released its heavy-duty Model 140 with a 12-horsepower Kohler engine and hydrostatic transmission. Marketing materials suggest that this ground-engaging machine would be most attractive to estate owners, vegetable growers, and nursery owners. It was a well-equipped tractor and came standard with hydraulic lift. In 1969, the 140 was repowered with Kohler's 14-horsepower single-cylinder engine and came with steering brakes. The tractor was discontinued in 1974.

As might be expected, these early John Deere garden tractors are extremely popular among collectors. Original odd-colored patio tractors can fetch a price that's several times their sticker.

Massey Ferguson

Massey Ferguson entered the suburban garden tractor market in the early 1960s with a predominantly yellow tractor called the MF 8 Executive. This machine looked like a scaled down utility tractor. The 510-pound Executive had an eight-horsepower Kohler engine that was coupled to a three-speed transaxle through a belt-

Massey Ferguson's MF 8 Executive was the company's first garden tractor. It sported yellow and white paint and laid the foundation for an excellent family of machines that would care for suburban lawns and gardens for several decades. *Author's collection*

idler clutch. Some references indicate that there was also a seven-horsepower version of the Executive.

Dura Corporation built the Executive line. This company was also responsible for the Moto-Mower and Porter Cable tractors, as well as others.

In 1966 and 1967, Massey Ferguson came out with a pair of garden tractors that were more in keeping with the style of its farm tractors of the day, the MF 10 and MF 12. Sometime in 1964, Massey Ferguson purchased Badger Northland, Inc., which was a company that focused on material handling of all kinds. Badger's forage harvester plant in Algoma, Wisconsin, became the new location for Massey Ferguson's garden tractor production. Company lore suggests that the reason garden tractor production moved there was to keep the town alive once forage harvester production was phased out.

The MF 10 was the first off the line at the old Badger plant. These tractors were powered with 10-horsepower Tecumseh engines and featured four-speed transaxles with variable-speed belt drives. The MF 10 was a stout little tractor that could push, pull, and power implements with the best of them. In 1967, the MF 10

Massey's MF 7 garden tractor came on line in 1968. It featured a belt-idler-type clutch (in the gear-drive models) and could be equipped with electric start.

Massey's MF 12 was a state-of-the-art variable-speed drive machine when it was released in 1967. The tractor is capable of pulling a single-bottom 12-inch plow under ideal soil conditions.

was joined by the MF 12, which was powered with a 12-horsepower Tecumseh engine and came standard with an infinitely variable hydrostatic drive. A modular hydraulic lift system became available the next year.

In 1968, the MF 7 came on line, and by 1969 it was joined with a MF 7 Hydra-Speed, which was Massey's name for the hydrostatic transmission. These tractors were likely never built at Algoma (in fact, they might have been built by American Machine & Foundry), as the entire garden tractor production moved to Des Moines in 1970. The garden tractor lineup then shared production space with Massey's Ski-Whiz snowmobile products.

Minneapolis-Moline

As part of its concerted efforts to diversify in the early 1960s, Minneapolis-Moline's Motec division entered the lawn and garden market in 1962 with a seven-horsepower

The MF 10 had a list price of around $900 by the late 1960s. Most folks spent quite a bit more than that by the time they outfitted the tractor with a nice complement of attachments.

The Jacobsen-built Mocraft garden tractor got Minneapolis-Moline into the garden tractor arena in the early 1960s. This machine was essentially a repainted Chief 100.

Minneapolis-Moline's Model 108 continues to captivate collectors young and old. This beautifully restored, Jacobsen-built machine has the eight-horsepower Kohler engine.

tractor and an impressive line of attachments to go with it. The tractors were, for the most part, production Chief 100 models built by Jacobsen. Initially, Moline's garden tractors were painted brown and wore the Mocraft badge on the sides of the hood.

The Mocraft tractor was sold from 1962 to 1963 and featured a Kohler engine with electric start. In keeping with Minneapolis-Moline's sound agricultural roots, the Mocraft garden tractors could be equipped with a PTO for powering grain elevators, augers, and generators, which the company pushed as a means to take advantage of tax breaks afforded to farm machinery.

In 1963, the Model 107 Town and Country came on line. Some say that this tractor replaced the Mocraft, although it was powered with only a 7-horsepower Tecumseh engine. In 1964, the Model 107 was joined by two other Town and Country models, which were named the Town and Country 108 and 110. These latter two tractors were powered with 8- and 10-horsepower Kohler engines, respectively (some references say the 108 had a Briggs & Stratton). Both new models had a 36-inch deck until 1966, when the Model 110 was equipped with a 42-inch deck. In 1966, the Model 110 could also be ordered with a hydrostatic transmission.

The Model 110 Town and Country was one of Minneapolis-Moline's most popular garden tractor models. Note the foot controls for the belt-idler clutch on this lovely specimen.

A new tractor, the Model 112, was also released in 1966. This was a deluxe tractor that offered 12-horsepower Kohler power and a choice of manual or hydrostatic transmissions. This little tractor was also available with several optional tire sizes and styles. In 1969, the Town and Country 114 was released. This 14-horsepower Kohler-powered tractor was available only with the hydrostatic transmission and offered a hydraulic or electric lift for raising and lowering mowers and other attachments. According to at least one reference, the 107, 108, 110, 112, and 114 Town and Country garden tractors remained in production into the early 1970s.

Colt and Case

Colt Manufacturing Company was the brainchild of Warren and Walter Johnson, and in 1961, they set out to build a sturdy four-wheel garden tractor from their Milwaukee, Wisconsin, location. Their initial efforts yielded a pair of gear-drive prototypes, but they quickly changed the design and released a pair of hydraulically driven machines in 1963.

By most measures, these tractors are considered to be the first hydraulically driven garden tractors to hit the market. It should be noted, however, that the transmission was not a true variable-displacement hydrostat. Instead, it consisted of a gear-type hydraulic pump plumbed through an infinitely variable control valve to an orbital hydraulic motor. In turn, the hydraulic motor drove the tractor's heavy-duty two-speed transaxle. This proprietary drive system was called the Colt-A-Matic (later known as Hy-Drive), and it proved robust in most conditions.

Those first models, the Colt 7 (with a 7-horsepower Kohler) and Colt 9 (with a 9.5-horsepower Kohler) were equipped with heavy cast-iron front grilles, cast-iron front axles, and Ross cam-and-follower-type steering gears.

The Colt 10 was among the first that the company produced after it was moved to Winneconne. Note the Colt-A-Matic hydraulic plumbing forward of the rear tire on this 1963 model.

This 1964 Colt 2310 was powered with a 10-horsepower Tecumseh engine and could be equipped with turf tires, as shown here, or bar-lug agricultural tires for better pulling in the field.

Hydraulic expanding-shoe drum brakes were available as an option. Like other brands of the day, the Colt tractors were available with a large number of attachments, including mowers, garden tools, a snow thrower, a grader blade, and a cart.

In response to economic incentives from the Winneconne Development Corporation, Colt moved its manufacturing and business operations to Winneconne, Wisconsin, in March 1963. The company was still producing the Colt 7 and Colt 9 models, but those produced at Winneconne were subtly different. Their serial tags and locations had changed, and the Winneconne-built models were equipped with ammeters.

By early 1964, the Colt lineup included the Colt 10 Deluxe, the Super, and the Rancher 10. The Colt 10 Deluxe was virtually identical to the Colt 9, except the company rounded up the horsepower to 10. The Colt Super came with a 10-horsepower engine, as did the Rancher 10, which was a high-clearance tractor and featured a heavier front axle with extended spindles and taller rear tires. The Rancher 10 was also unique because it came standard with an hydraulic oil cooler, which was particularly important when the hydraulically driven machines pulled ground-engaging equipment. Some references indicate that 12-horsepower versions of these same machines also were available.

Case purchased Colt in late 1964 and used the wholly owned subsidiary to produce garden tractors with the Case name on them. Colt continued to build machines for its independent dealers through 1966. Later Colt models included the 130, 180, 150, 190, 2110, and several others.

Case marketed both Case and Colt brand garden tractors for a few years after purchasing Colt Manufacturing Company. The earliest Case garden tractors were likely the 130 and 180, which were ready for the 1965 model year. The Case 120, 150, and 190 were built during the 1966 model year; the latter two were renamed the Model 155 and 195 for 1967. The 155 was powered with Kohler's K-241A 10-horsepower engine, while the 195 used Kohler's 12-horsepower K301A. The 195 had slightly more ground clearance as well. These machines both used disc brakes.

By the end of the decade, Case's garden tractor lineup included the 155 and 195, as well as Models 220, 222, 442, and 444. The Model 220 and 222 were virtually identical except that they were powered with Kohler's 10- and 12-horsepower engines, respectively. The same could be said for the higher ground clearance 12-horsepower Model 442 and 14-horsepower 444. These six Case garden tractor models were all the company offered into the early 1970s.

Bolens

Bolens entered the 1960s with quite a few walking tractor models and at least a couple of Ride-A-Matics. In 1960, the Ride-A-Matic 230 was replaced with the 231

With its 14-horsepower engine, hydraulic lift, and hydraulic drive, this 1969 Case Model 444 was born to work. This tractor could be equipped with everything from mowing decks to land plows to front-end loader attachments.

and 232. These tractors were both powered with Kohler's single-cylinder seven-horsepower cast-iron K161 engine, and both weighed about 500 pounds. The principal difference between the two machines is that the Model 232 offered electric start.

The next year, these two tractors were sold as the Ride-A-Matic Models 233 and 234. Again, the 234 had electric start. Both were rated to pull a single 8- to 10-inch bottom plow, depending on soil type and condition. This was also the last year for Bolens' two-wheeled tractors.

In 1962, the 233 and 234 were replaced with the Ride-A-Matic 235 and 236, and a pair of six-horsepower Briggs & Stratton–powered riding garden tractors joined the force. These Huski 600 Models 180 and 181 offered manual or electric starting, respectively. Both also had a three-speed dual-range transmission system. These 500-pound machines were slightly smaller than the Ride-A-Matic line, and both could be fit with all manner of attachments to make life in suburbia easy to contend with.

The 1962 Bolens Model 1000 sported a very stylish brown-and-white color scheme that was every bit as stunning as the 10-horsepower workhorse was capable.

In 1962, Bolens replaced the heavy cast grille with one made of sheet metal on most of its tractors. This 1962 Model 600 awaits its new decals.

By the early 1960s, Bolens had changed its color scheme from green to gold, as illustrated by this 1961 Model 233.

The Ride-A-Matic line was discontinued by 1963, when the Huski 600 (with a 6-horsepower Briggs & Stratton) and 800 (with a 7.25-horsepower Wisconsin) models were available. Both tractors were available with electric or manual starting and represent some of the earliest versions of a new tube-frame-style tractor. These machines were updated for 1966 as the 650 (with a 6-horsepower Briggs & Stratton) and 850 (with a 8.25-horsepower Wisconsin). The 10-horsepower Wisconsin-powered Model 1050 also joined the line that year. By then, the 850 and 1050 were available with electric start only.

In 1967, the 650 was upgraded to the 7-horsepower Briggs & Stratton–powered 750. The 850 and 1050 remained largely unchanged, but a unique gradual-locking differential, known as the Controlled Differential, was available on the 850 and 1050 models. A 12-horsepower Wisconsin-powered 1250 also was released that year. This tractor offered electric starting and an Eaton hydrostatic drive system. This half-ton monster was built on a larger channel-style steel frame, which was a significant departure from the tube-style frame of the others. In 1968, the Model 770 replaced the 750. The 770 was powered with a seven-horsepower Briggs & Stratton engine and was constructed with a new, smaller, boxed frame.

By the end of the decade, Bolens' garden tractor lineup included the electric- and manual-start versions of the 770, 775 (a 770 with six-speed transmission), 850, 1050, 1220, 1225, 1250, and several other higher-powered models. The Model 1220 used a 12-horsepower Lauson engine and offered six forward speeds, while the 1225 used a 12-horsepower Wisconsin engine and an Eaton transmission. The 14-horsepower Wisconsin-powered 1455 tractor was the highest-powered garden tractor Bolens offered in 1969.

Bush Hog

Perhaps better known for its incredible rotary cutters and rough-country mowers, Bush Hog began selling garden tractors built by Shaw Manufacturing in Kansas as early as 1962. By the end of that year, Bush Hog, based in Selma, Alabama, owned Shaw. It appears that Bush Hog sold garden tractors for the next 10 years or so. But in the early 1970s, when it got out of the business, Bush Hog evidently destroyed virtually all the serial number lists and other traces of that aspect of its business. In fact, current Bush Hog corporate public relations material doesn't even mention the Shaw connection.

Even though the build dates for the various Bush Hog garden tractors can't be pinpointed, the models and their fundamental features can be described. Early on, the company offered a T-63 tractor, which was powered with a seven-horsepower Wisconsin engine that was shaft-

Bush Hog's D4-10 was built in Kansas at the Shaw plant. The machine had a four-speed gear-drive transaxle with a 10-horsepower Wisconsin engine.

coupled to a two-speed dual-range transmission. The little tractor had four forward speeds and a pair of reverses. The T-63 differs from the later seven-horsepower gear-drive D4-7 in a few places, such as the front axle. The T-63 has a dropped axle compared with the D4-7.

The D4-7 was in production with the D4-10, which was powered with a 10-horsepower Wisconsin engine in a package that was very similar to its lower-powered sibling. While these machines lacked many operator amenities, they were equipped with a live rear PTO, and, as might be expected, Bush Hog made a small trailing rotary cutter that these tractors could pull and power.

The D4-10 was still in production in 1969, and it was listed with several Vari-Drive machines that used a variable belt drive and Peerless transaxle to transmit power from the engine to the rear wheels. The VR3-6 (with a six-horsepower Tecumseh manual start) and VE3-6 (same as VR3-6 with electric start) each had a three-speed transaxle. The VE4-6 (with a six-horsepower Tecumseh) and VE4-7 (with a seven-horsepower Wisconsin) had the Peerless four-speed creeper transmission.

Under Bush Hog's ownership, the Shaw factory produced several models with hydrostatic transmissions too.

JACOBSEN: A LATE ENTRY INTO THE MARKET

Jacobsen was late in coming out with a four-wheeled garden tractor. By the time it got there in the early 1960s, the company had been in business for over a quarter of a century. Founded in 1921, the company produced self-propelled or tractor-pulled reel-type mowers that were particularly attractive to the golf and turf industries. The company is responsible for manufacturing the first golf course greens mower.

The Jacobsen Manufacturing Company traces its roots to a Danish craftsman, Knud Jacobsen, who arrived in Racine, Wisconsin, in 1891. Family history indicates that Knud was, from the very beginning, artistic and especially creative with his hands. An accomplished woodworker at a very young age, Knud found work in Racine as a fine furniture maker. Soon he was being sought out for his patterns.

By the turn of the twentieth century, he had opened his own company, Jacobsen Manufacturing Company, which was principally a pattern-making shop. He played an important role in the burgeoning agricultural, automotive, and electrical industries of the day. He even produced engine patterns for companies like Harley Davidson and J. I. Case, among many others.

In 1917, Jacobsen reorganized as Thor Machine Works, and by 1921, with a little help from engineer friend A. J. Dremel, the company released the 4-Acre mower, one of the very first mowers to be powered with a gasoline engine. Today, this mower would be described as a self-propelled reel mower. The 4-Acre spawned decades of estate and golf course mower development. Interestingly, the 4-Acre was marketed through Jacobsen Manufacturing, not Thor Machine Works.

After surviving the Depression relatively intact, Knud retired in 1939, and his son Oscar soon took over as president. By this time, the company was thinking about manufacturing homeowner-sized mowers. After contributing its fair share to the war effort, Jacobsen entered the homeowner market through an earlier acquisition of the Johnston Lawn Mower Company of Ottumwa, Iowa. This relationship evolved into Jacobsen's consumer products division. By the 1950s, the company offered reel-type and rotary-type lawnmowers for the consumer market. By the end of that decade, the Javelin, a riding mower, was ready for market. A few years later, the Jacobsen Chief garden tractor was introduced.

After a long and successful run that included manufacturing garden tractors for the likes of Minneapolis-Moline, Oliver, Ford, Cockshutt, Homelite, and others, Jacobsen was purchased by Textron in about 1975. Still, Jacobsen and Jacobsen/Homelite garden tractors were produced into at least the 1990s. Today, the company is principally concerned with professional turf maintenance machinery.

These tractors were also equipped with hydraulic implement lifts. Models HD-10 and HW-10 had 10-horsepower Tecumseh engines, while the HD-12 and HW-12 came with 12-horsepower motors from the same manufacturer. Hydrostatic models JB-1 and JB-2 (also called Javelina I and Javelina II) were more akin to true subcompact farm tractors and came with three-point hitches and live rear PTOs. By 1969, the Javelina I had a 14-horsepower Kohler and weighed 1,050 pounds; the Javelina II—the Javelina I's 12-horsepower Briggs & Stratton–powered sibling—tipped the scales at only 870 pounds.

Bush Hog tractors are highly collectible today because of their connection to Shaw and brief production life.

Jacobsen

Jacobsen entered the four-wheel garden tractor market with the seven-horsepower Tecumseh-powered Chief in the early 1960s. In 1962, *Implement and Tractor's Red Tractor Book* lists two Jacobsen Chief models: the standard 100-A and deluxe 100-B. Both were powered with Kohler's K-161 seven-horsepower engine, but the 100B had electric starting. These garden tractors were both rated to pull a single 10-inch plow bottom.

By 1965, Jacobsen had several new models, including the Chief 100-G, which was listed as a deluxe 9.5-horsepower Kohler-powered version of the 7-horsepower (Kohler) Chief 100-C and 100-D models. These tractors featured belt-idler clutches and three-speed transmissions with a single reverse. Options included electric start, several front-mounted reel mowers, and other attachments that would make the little tractor a year-round workhorse.

By 1967, the company sales literature listed the 8-horsepower Chief 800, 10-horsepower Chief 1000, and 12-horsepower Chief 1200. All were gear driven and all were Kohler powered. At the same time, a pair of Super Chief tractors was also available. These tractors were deluxe models that included upgraded seats and hydrostatic transmissions, among other amenities. By 1969, a 16-horsepower model was added to the mix.

Early Jacobsen garden tractors, especially those produced for other manufacturers, are among the most sought-after collectibles in the lawn and garden market.

Ford

Ford entered the garden tractor market in the mid-1960s with a two-member lineup from Jacobsen: the Ford 80 and 100 models. These were nearly identical to Jacobsen's variously powered Chief 100 models. In 1966, Ford added its version of the Chief 1200, which was called the Ford 120. This machine was powered with a 12-horsepower Kohler engine and featured a hydrostatic transmission.

The following year, the lineup included 8-, 10-, and 12-horsepower gear-drive tractors and 10- or 12-horsepower models with hydrostatic transmissions. In the last year of the decade, the 8- and 10-horsepower gear drives were discontinued, and a 14-horsepower hydro was added.

David Bradley

Sears continued to offer garden tractors with the David Bradley name through 1964. Initially, the company offered the David Bradley Suburban in 1960 and 1961, in a package that was virtually unchanged from the 1959 version. The Suburban 575 (powered by a 5.75-horsepower Briggs & Stratton) was released in 1962 as a machine that was virtually identical to the first Suburbans, except that its grille was redesigned and included cooling slots. The tractor came standard

By 1962, Jacobsen's Chief 100 models offered several innovative attachments to make the tractors more interesting to farmers and to help the machines qualify for tax breaks. The 540-rpm PTO shown here was one such option. *Author's collection*

Ford's Model 100 garden tractor was pretty much a repainted Jacobsen Chief 100. Note the headlight placement on this beautifully restored machine.

without brakes or electric start, although both could be added.

The Suburban 725—a 7.25-horsepower Briggs & Stratton–powered machine with more modern styling than its lower-powered sibling—joined the Suburban 575 that same year. This tractor came standard with independent brakes on the rear axle. In 1963, the Suburban 575 was renamed the Suburban 600, but it was essentially the same tractor as the 575. The next year's Suburban 600 took on the more modern styling of the Suburban 725, and in 1965 they were joined by the more capable Suburban 8 and Suburban 10 tractors. These machines offered 8- and 10-horsepower respectively, in addition to significantly more modern styling and features.

In the mid-1960s, Sears dropped the David Bradley transmissions in favor of the readily available transaxles of the day. The 12-horsepower Suburban 12 was released in 1966 and the Super 12 in 1967. By the end of the decade, Sears offered several garden tractors that were still capable of performing ground-engaging work. Interestingly, David Bradley's new owner, Roper, built many of the machines.

Sears continues to offer lawn and garden tractors today, and through the years Roper and several other manufacturers have built them.

Engineering Products Company

Throughout the 1960s, Engineering Products Company offered two lines of Economy tractors, one known as the Jim Dandy and the other as the Power King. Initially,

Ariens offered the Manorway riding tractor by the end of the 1960s. This machine was really classified as a lawn tractor, but it could be fit with a snow blade.

the Jim Dandy came equipped with a 9-horsepower engine (which was a Wisconsin powerplant before 1961, then a Briggs & Stratton). The little tractor could be equipped with sufficient attachments to make it useful around the estate and the small farm. By mid-decade, the 9-horsepower engine had been upgraded to Kohler's 10-horsepower unit. By the end of the decade, 12- and 14-horsepower Kohler-powered Jim Dandy tractors had been released.

The Economy Power King lineup also entered the decade with a 9-horsepower model, which came in two different variations, the 8-16 and 8-24 (named for the size of their rear tires). By mid-decade, 10-horsepower Power Kings had been released; 12- and

14-horsepower tractors soon followed. By the end of the decade, at least two different trim levels were available: standard and deluxe. The differences were primarily in sheet metal and other cosmetics.

COPAR Panzer

Under Virginia Metalcrafters' early guidance, the larger three-wheeled and four-wheeled Panzer garden tractors were dropped from the lineup in the early 1960s, while the lighter line was redesigned. And perhaps more notably, this redesign included the switch to the familiar turquoise paint job and a grille whose badge simply read "Panzer." This model consolidation, coupled with a nice array of attachments, increased the brand's mar-

The Speedex S-24 utilized the company's interesting gear and belt drivetrain, but that never kept it from excelling at ground-engaging work.

ket share substantially. The Panzer models now included the T70, T70ES, T70B, T70B-ES, and T707ES and spanned the years 1961 to 1963.

In 1964, after Virginia Metalcrafters' acquisition of Pennsylvania Lawn Products, the so-called Pennsylvania Panzers included some transitional Model T70 machines and an updated lineup that included the T75, T758, and T758ES. These tractors were styled like the predecessors, with rounded hoods. From about 1966 through the end of production in the early 1970s, several Panzer models with updated sheet metal were built. These included Model 1008 (8 horsepower), 1010 (10 horsepower), 1010a, 1012 (12 horsepower), 1012a, 1107 (7 horsepower), and 1110R (10 horsepower). These tractors were powered with either Tecumseh or Briggs & Stratton engines (model dependent), and offered three speeds forward with a single reverse or hydrostatic transmission, and electric or recoil starting.

Simplicity

In 1960, Simplicity's first four-wheel garden tractor was renamed to avoid confusion with the company's line of Wonderboy rear-engine riding mowers. The Wonderboy 700 lost the Wonderboy moniker to become the Simplicity 700. In 1961, that first garden tractor received a slightly more powerful 7.25-horsepower engine and was renamed the Simplicity 725. This model, with a yellow paint job and some minor sheet-metal reworking, was also sold as the Allis-Chalmers B-1. The stout little 725 could be equipped with several sizes and types of mowers, a 32-inch rotary tiller, a 10-inch moldboard plow, and many other attachments.

By 1964, the 725 had evolved into the 9-horsepower Briggs & Stratton–powered Landlord tractor. The company introduced its Broadmoor line of lawn tractors that same year. In 1965, the Landlord received a 10-horsepower engine and was renamed the Landlord 101. In 1966, the 12-horsepower Sovereign was introduced. This deluxe tractor featured electric starting, hydraulic lift, and other operator amenities.

In 1967, Simplicity garden tractors sported a redesigned and somewhat more angular hood. The 10-horsepower and 12-horsepower Landlord 2010 and 2012 both offered hydraulic lift, easy-spin electric starting, front, mid, and rear PTOs, and a whole range of implements and attachments. By the end of the decade, the company had

In 1963, Wheel Horse's Model 603 featured a forward-mounted engine and the company's proprietary transaxle. Note the unusual steering wheel on this beautifully restored machine.

several 10- and 12-horsepower tractors, including the 12-horsepower 3212H hydrostatic-drive Sovereign.

Speedex

In 1960, Speedex offered three tractors to the growing garden tractor market, including the 3-horsepower two-wheeled S-8, the 5.75-horsepower S-14, and the 9-horsepower S-23. All used Briggs & Stratton engines, and the four-wheeled S-14 and S-23 were billed as fun, efficient, and versatile workhorses. The S-14 was physically smaller than the S-23, but both were rated for ground-engaging tools befitting any quality garden tractor of the day.

Speedex continued to offer the S-23 through 1966 and the S-14 through 1968. Both tractors went through a number of series upgrades over the years. For example, by 1962, the S-14 was a six-horsepower tractor with an upgraded transmission. The machines featured cast-steel final drive gears, welded steel frames, and sliding-engine-type belt-tightener clutches. Both models could be fit with an array of Unit-Design tools that mounted easily and were built to agricultural standards.

In 1966, the S-23 was replaced with the S-24. This tractor was powered with a 10-horsepower Briggs & Stratton engine and offered several forward speeds with its combination belt and gear transmission drive system.

In 1968, the S-1 replaced the S-17 and the new S-18 was added to the line. The S-17 was powered with a seven-horsepower Briggs & Stratton engine, while the S-18 had an eight-horsepower Kohler. The S-17 had the more conventional Speedex transmission system, while the S-18 offered a true four-speed (five-speed in some references) system. By the end of the decade, these three tractors continued to serve Speedex's sales needs well. All three were listed in the 1969 *Implement and Tractor Red Book*.

Wheel Horse

The 1960s were good for Wheel Horse. From the get go, the company offered an expanded and improved line. In 1960, for example, Wheel Horse released an improved Ride-Away Junior with a redesigned steering system and more functional implement lift, not to mention updated sheet metal and many other improvements. The tractor was offered as the four- and five-horsepower Suburban 400 and Suburban 550, respectively.

In 1961, the Suburban 400 was renamed the 401, the 550 was renamed the 551, and an all-new Model 701 was released. The 551 received an improved Uni-Drive case that year, but the tractor was essentially the same as the 550. The Suburban 701 was unusual for Wheel Horse because its engine was located up front instead of in the mid position, a design that all of the company's tractors (except the Ride-Away Senior) had. The 701 also could be equipped with an expanded line of tools, many of which were specially designed for it.

By 1963, the Wheel Horse lineup was truly extensive. From the diminutive Lawn Ranger, which was essentially a garden tractor with smaller wheels, to the 9.6-horsepower Model 953, the company had the entire range of garden tractors covered. The Models 603, 633, 653, and 753 pretty much shared the same engine-forward chassis found on the earlier 701. The 953 was larger overall.

In 1964, Wheel Horse added a couple of Lawn Ranger models and replaced the 1963 lineup with Models 604, 654, 704, 854, and 1054. The following year, the

company's offerings underwent a major facelift that included a new, more modern-looking hood. The older rounded hood was still used on the Lawn Rangers, but the new models—the 605, 655, 855, 1045, and 1055—all got the new look. The Model 1045 had the new hood but the older-style fenders, while the others had new fenders and a new hood. All came with Wheel Horse's Uni-Drive transmission.

Wheel Horse's big news for 1965 came in the form of a pair of hydraulically driven tractors. These so-called automatic-drive machines featured a lever-operated direction and speed control. Initially available as 8- and 10-horsepower units, the Models 875 and 1075 Wheel-A-Matics made garden tractor history as the first hydraulically driven (but not truly hydrostatic) production machines to hit the market.

In 1966, Wheel Horse offered gear-drive Models 606, 656, 856, and 1056. Wheel-A-Matic models included the 8-horsepower 876, 10-horsepower 1076, and 12-horsepower 1276. The gear-drive machines were updated in 1967 to the Models 607, 657, 857, and 1057. Also, a 12-horsepower 1257 was added to the line. Wheel-A-Matic tractors were updated to the Models 877, 1077, and 1277. That year was also marked with the addition of the 867, 1067, and 1267, all of which came with a dual-range three-speed gear transmission, which made the perfect partners for rotary tilling and other slow-going chores.

In 1968, Wheel Horse's lineup changed considerably. The lower-powered garden tractors included the Commando models. These tractors typically had three- speed Uni-Drive transmissions and eight or less horsepower. The six-speed gear-driven Raider and Wheel-A-Matic-driven Charger machines all had nine or more horsepower. There was also an Electro-12 available, which was essentially a 12-horsepower Charger equipped with an electric PTO clutch.

By the end of the decade, Wheel Horse offered Commando, Workhorse, Raider, Charger, and Electro-12 models, in addition to a completely new 14-horsepower GT-14 that would set the stage for the 1970s and beyond.

REDESIGNING THE CUB CADET

International's first garden tractor (released in January 1961) was simply called the Cub Cadet and was the product of a rapid development program that went from concept to production in little over a year's time.

"The product [was] a greater success than anyone had dreamed of," said Harold Schramm, the driveline engineer on the project. The Cub Cadet (now called the Original to distinguish it from later numbered models) went through some minor changes during its production life, but it utilized a seven-horsepower Kohler engine, a V-belt to couple the engine to the clutch driveshaft, and a U-spring-mounted pan seat throughout. The Cub Cadet was so successful that in spite of the belt in the drivetrain and the fact that frame-to-transmission mount tabs often cracked when heavily used, the company felt no need to remake the line. Nevertheless, International Harvester's Industrial Equipment Group did push to restyle the machine shortly after it was released.

According to concept engineer Keith Burnham, the tooling for the Cub Cadet was never designed to handle the production numbers that it eventually saw. For example, near the end, its frame-stamping machinery was worn enough that line workers accomplished final frame shaping with sledgehammers. Burnham notes that for that reason alone, the company had to change the Cub Cadet to some degree by 1963. In the end, the process yielded a vastly improved machine that really put the Cub Cadet garden tractor on the map.

Orchestrating Change

"Change is never easy for some people," Keith Burnham said. "But I like to change things because you can always make them better." While truer words were likely never spoken, even Burnham admits that there was some internal competition within IH's engineering units for the right to take the lead on the Cub Cadet's redesign. In the end, the project came out of IH's Advanced Engineering Group at the Farm Equipment Division's Hinsdale Engineering Center, although Burnham provided some drawings for the Industrial Design Group as well. "I was always looking for the next project," he said. "So when [the] industrial design [people] needed some detail of its proposal drawn, they asked me to do it."

Early concept proposals for the new, "improved" Cub Cadet that came out of the Industrial Design Group by late 1961 took two general approaches. The first concepts were tendered and drawn specifically by W. D. Syrett. These maintained the V-belt driveline link between the engine and clutch shaft and incorporated styling features that were very obviously borrowed directly from competitive garden tractor manufacturers, such as Simplicity, Bolens, and even Wheel Horse. To make it interesting, these concepts also considered using other IH paint colors, including blues and greens borrowed from the Motor Truck Division.

The second approach to a fresh Cub Cadet style retained the trademark yellow-and-white coloring and offered a V-belt-driven system with a sloped and tapered hood on what appears to be a largely unchanged chassis.

Neither of these approaches was seriously considered because they didn't make significant mechanical improvements to the Cub Cadet's mechanical systems.

The Advanced Engineering Group submitted its new Cub Cadet proposal in early 1962 and completed the design by the end of that year.

Implementing Change

At a large outdoor power products show in January 1962, the head of IH's Advanced Engineering Group saw a Bolens garden tractor utilizing a U-joint and shaft-driven mower deck, which eliminated the long, twisted mule drive belt that most manufacturers (including IH) had been using to power garden

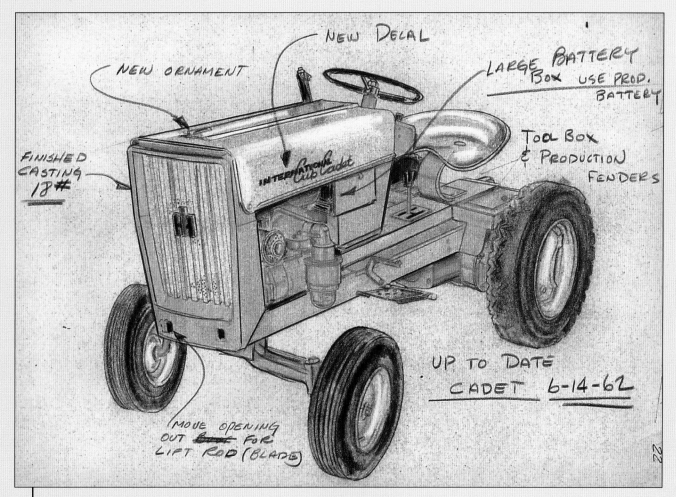

NEW DECAL

NEW ORNAMENT

LARGE BATTERY BOX USE PROD. BATTERY

TOOL BOX & PRODUCTION FENDERS

FINISHED CASTING 18#

INTERNATIONAL Cub Cadet

UP TO DATE CADET 6-14-62

MOVE OPENING OUT ~~B~~ FOR LIFT ROD (BLADE)

This concept drawing is one of scores that were produced as part of the first Cub Cadet redesign process. That effort ultimately gave rise to the Models 70 and 100. *Author's collection*

tractor–mounted mower decks from the front of the engine. As a result, Harold Schramm, a member of the design group, was assigned the task of designing a U-joint shaft drive for Cub Cadet mowers. His first step was to visit an IH dealer in Elgin, Illinois, which was also a Bolens dealer, to look the competitive model over and take some measurements.

In order to fit the shaft-driven mower, the Cub Cadet's frame needed to be raised to improve undercarriage clear-

ance. The design team's solution was to build an upturned channel frame with two parallel rails that would bolt to the sides of the transmission and above the axle-carrier tubes. That single change strengthened the frame-to-transaxle connection and allowed the seven-horsepower engine to be mounted low enough that the crankshaft aligned directly with the clutch and driveshaft. The clutch was no longer off-center, and thus IH could eliminate a belt from the drivetrain.

"The original Cadet met the requirements for a tractor as far as design specifications were concerned; however, the belt drive detracted from the feeling that it was a true tractor," Schramm explained as further motivation for looking toward a change to direct drive.

The new frame and drivetrain alignment also meant that the steering gear needed to be relocated slightly to the left of center, which had the team members worried about the tractor's aesthetics. With Keith Burnham's styling and concept design skills, they needn't have worried, though, and most enthusiasts today don't even realize that the steering wheel is a little to the left.

The group still faced one last vexing hurdle. The trend with competing garden tractors was toward more horsepower, and the team felt that the Kohler single-cylinder 10-horsepower powerplant was ideal for the project. Unfortunately, the engine wouldn't fit between the frame rails, and Kohler didn't want to modify the 10-horsepower engine's base because of cooling and lubrication concerns. After considerable discussion and testing, the IH team convinced Kohler to change its 10-horsepower engine's mounting base so that it would fit in the new, narrow frame chassis.

Once the power and drivetrain fundamentals were worked out, completing the new Cub Cadet's styling took a bit more wrangling in a process of give and take that netted several premockup drawings and associated mockup tractors. Everything from hubcaps and toolboxes to fenders, seats, steering wheels, the operator's station, sheet metal, and even the hood ornament underwent staged evolution before the look was considered right.

"After a series of modifications to the concept, we would go and redo the mockup," Burnham said of the process. "Sometimes the changes were incorporated by producing a new casting; sometimes we just made new parts out of wood."

In the end, the styling changes included a new grille, hood, pedestal, and fenders, as well as a new brake system and driveline when the Cub Cadet Model 70 and Model 100 were released in August 1963. Ironically, these models did not come with the shaft-driven mower the tractor's design had been initially planned around. It had proved too expensive to manufacture.

By the time this second series Cub Cadet left production in August 1965, its two-year run had netted almost 62,000 delivered units. Corporate records indicate that of that substantial total, about 22,600 were Model 70s. Clearly the 10-horsepower engine was a well-received improvement.

Developing a Classic in Retrospect

Neither Burnham nor Schramm, nor the rest of the Advanced Engineering Group, could have known that they were in the midst of developing one of the most durable and now highly collectible garden tractors of all time when struggling through the Model 100's design process. Instead, like virtually all engineers, they were juggling issues related to aesthetics, mechanical ability, durability, and production economy as they developed the concept. In the end, they created a heavy-duty second-generation Cub Cadet tractor that is every bit as capable at 40-plus years of age as it was when first delivered. Hundreds of the little tractors are still on the job, while many more are sequestered away in private collections. The Model 100's frame and fundamental styling provided the basis for the next decade of Cub Cadet evolution at International Harvester.

The final mockup resulting from the first Cub Cadet redesign. The tractors were ultimately called the Models 70 and 100. In the final production version, the openings at the bottom of the grille were not included.
Author's collection

The Bolens Husky 1256 and 1257 featured single-foot-pedal control of the hydrostatic transmission (both direction and speed) and a shaft-driving PTO, unlike most others of the day, which used mule belts to power the implement. *Author's collection*

CHAPTER
4

REFINING THE LINES
(1970–1979)

After years of sustained economic expansion, the 1970s began with a series of recessions that culminated in some of the highest interest rates in American history. As the cost of money, labor, and energy steadily rose, so did the cost of producing lawn and garden equipment. Early in the decade, the war in Vietnam was on the minds of most Americans. As the years passed, the Arab oil embargo, Watergate, and a myriad of other issues plagued the country.

In spite of it all, folks were still moving to suburbia in droves, and they all needed machines to help with their maintenance chores. Still, with all the economic uncertainty, the garden tractor arena saw some consolidation among manufacturers. It also saw the development of some very sophisticated machines.

Allis-Chalmers

In 1970, the Allis-Chalmers garden tractor lineup included the Simplicity-built 10-horsepower, electric-start, gear-drive B-210 in power- and manual-lift versions, a similar pair of gear-driven 12-horsepower B-212 machines, and a pair of 12-horsepower hydrostatic-transmission H-212 tractors, with either manual or power lifts.

In 1971, Allis-Chalmers offered three 14-horsepower garden tractors, three 12-horsepower units, and two 10-horsepower models. By then, the tractor manufacturer also listed several lower horsepower lawn tractors in its product literature. At the top of the list was the Model 314H, a 14-horsepower hydrostatic-drive tractor with electric lift and electric PTO (engagement). The Model 314D was a deluxe version of the 14-horsepower Kohler-powered 314. The 314D used the same Vari-Shift manual transmission as the 314, but it also offered electric lift and electric PTO.

The Models 312, 312D, and 312H were similarly equipped to their 314 counterparts, with the most notable difference in the 12-horsepower Kohler engine. At the low end of the range for the Allis-Chalmers–labeled Simplicity garden tractors, the Models 310 and 310D came equipped with only 10-horsepower Kohler engines.

By the early 1970s, Simplicity had created a hydrostatic-drive tractor to compete with IH's estate-oriented 154 Cub LoBoy, and in 1972, Allis-Chalmers offered the Model 616 as a result of that effort. The 616 was considered a small agricultural or utility tractor by some folks, but it was a great little acreage machine. The 616 had a larger frame than the other garden

An early 1970s Allis-Chalmers Model 410. This Simplicity-built machine has the optional four-speed shuttle transmission.

tractors and was styled like the 190 farm tractor. The Simplicity version of the 616 was called the Powermax, although it had different paint and hood. This 16.5-horsepower Onan twin cylinder-powered tractor offered hydrostatic drive with three gear-selected ranges. It had a Category 0 three-point and rear PTO standard.

In 1973, the 300 Series garden tractors were replaced with an updated 400 Series lineup: the Models 410, 414, and 416. The 10-horsepower 410 came standard with a three-speed gear transmission, but it could be optionally equipped with a four-speed forward and four-speed reverse shuttle transmission. The 14-horsepower 414 came standard with the shuttle drive, but an optional hydrostatic drive was also available. The 416's transmission options were essentially the same as on the 414. The Model 616's engine offered increased power and was renamed the 620. That tractor evolved into the Model 720 in 1975 and was virtually unchanged except in its decals.

During the Nixon administration, the government relaxed most of its fair-trade laws, so Allis-Chalmers no longer had a legal need for the Lexington plant to retain

The 16-horsepower Allis-Chalmers Model 716 was available with a hydrostatic transmission (shown here) or six-speed gear drive.

For 1977, the company introduced the 800 Series garden tractors as an all-new line that included the 8-horsepower Model 808GT and 10-horsepower Model 810GT. Both were equipped with a three-speed transmission that was designed just for the series, and both used Briggs & Stratton engines. The Model 808GT was slightly slower in all gears (at top rpm) because of slightly smaller drive wheels. The 810GT had a shipping weight of about 590 pounds compared with the 808GT's 520. The tractors shared a chassis. An 11-horsepower Model 811GT was also listed prior to the end of the decade in at least one reference.

In 1979, the 900 Series tractors were introduced, along with an updated lineup of 800 Series machines. Included in the 800 Series now was the 16-horsepower twin-cylinder-powered Model 816GT. The 900 Series included the 10-, 12-, 14-, 16-, and 17-horsepower Kohler-powered Models 910 (with mechanical lift and six-speed transmission), 912 (with mechanical lift and hydrostatic transmission), 912H (912 with hydraulic lift), 914 (mechanical lift with shuttle transmission), 916 (with six-speed transmission), 916H (with hydrostatic transmission), and 917H (17-horsepower hydrostatic transmission). These tractors carried over into the 1980s.

International Harvester Cub Cadet

International Harvester engineer Harold Schramm said that by 1970, the Cub Cadet lineup's redesign had been on a roughly 24-month cycle. So the popular model began the 1970s virtually unchanged from 1969. With consumers clamoring for larger engines and the competition ever eager to oblige, International Harvester wasn't about to be left behind. The change that ensued was significant enough to ensure the tractor maker wouldn't be.

"Once the fender change was made on the 73-147 line, the frame change was not difficult," Schramm said about the beginning of the wide-frame Cub Cadet lines. "The new formed-steel frame had more space, and it also made the tractor look beefier."

This sixth line of garden tractors was introduced in late 1971 with Models 86, 108, 109, 128, 129, and 149.

Simplicity. As a result, the Lexington plant closed in 1973, and the tractors produced there were discontinued.

In 1974, Allis-Chalmers came out with its 700 Series garden tractors to replace the 400 Series garden tractor models (yet some 400 Series lawn tractor models were still in production). The lineup included an entry-level 10-horsepower, three-speed, gear-driven Model 710 in a fresh design that looked even more like the company's larger farm tractors of the day. The midrange Model 712 offered 12 horsepower and a choice of shuttle or hydrostatic drive. The high-end Model 716 was offered only with a hydrostatic transmission. Styling included headlights mounted on the sides of the grille housing.

In 1976, updated versions of the 700 Series garden tractors were released. For this year, the headlights had been moved inside the grille, a six-speed transmission replaced the three-speed on the Model 710, and a six-speed gear-drive Model 716 was added. In 1978, the 716 was replaced with a Model 718 (still powered by a 16-horsepower Kohler), offered with a hydrostatic transmission only.

The Model 169 was introduced near the end of the run in August 1974, and most appear to have been built in September and October. The tractors got new hoods, grilles, instrument panels, and many safety and convenience updates. Of course, the frame was wider up front to accommodate larger engines. For the first time, the grille casting was painted white, and the grille was now black plastic.

The gear-drive models—the 86, 108, and 128—used the International Cub's transmission. The other models were hydrostatic, including the 169—the first with a 16-horsepower engine. All models used the Cub's cast-iron rear-end housing and differential. The hydrostatic pumps on the two highest horsepower Cub Cadets were fitted with auxiliary ports to serve the lifting and/or remote hydraulic needs of the machines.

In the fall of 1974, IH introduced a new series called the Quietline. These wide-frame Cub Cadets had a new numbering scheme, rubber isolation of the engine from the frame, and an enclosed engine compartment. Initially, the Quietline Series included three gear-drive units in 8-, 10-, and 12-horsepower tractors, called the 800, 1000, and 1200, respectively. The 1250, 1450, and 1650 were the 12-, 14-, and 16-horsepower hydrostatic models. All still had Kohler engines; however, in order to remain competitive in the lower price range, IH introduced the Model 1100 later.

The Model 1100 was a significant deviation from the rest of the wide-frame Cub Cadets. IH dropped the International Cub transaxle, opting for a less-expensive four-speed Peerless brand transaxle, which was standard for most competing models. The Peerless transaxle employed a belt-idler-type clutch. The 1100 was powered by an 11-horsepower Briggs & Stratton engine, and to further cut costs, engine compartment side panels were not included—meaning that it was not a true Quietline.

Although it was not planned this way, the process to redesign the Cub Cadet that began again in 1977 would be the last time the popular model was upgraded. In 1979, its most profitable year ever, IH introduced the significantly redesigned line of Cub Cadets. The trac-

The Model 982, the flagship of IH's eighth series of Cub Cadets, had a larger super-garden tractor chassis and offered such amenities as Category 0 three-point hitch, steering brakes, and power steering.

tors were updated with safety and comfort changes, enhanced hydraulics, as well as many more engine choices. Styling included an all-enclosed engine compartment. IH painted the new Cub Cadets red after 19 years of yellow and white and again changed the numbering scheme.

The red 82 Series Cub Cadets included an 11-horsepower gear-drive Model 482 and 16-horsepower gear-drive Model 582. Both gear-drive tractors were offered with Briggs & Stratton engines, but only the 582 had the Cub transmission and differential. The 17-horsepower twin-cylinder Kohler-powered hydrostatic models were the 682 and 782. The largest tractor in the lineup was the 19-horsepower Model 982 tractor (later called Super Garden Tractor). It was based on a longer frame than the other members of the 82 Series and featured an optional Category 0 three-point hitch.

The last Cub Cadet built by International was most likely a Model 782, serial No. 694248. It came off

Among the first of the so-called wide-frame Cub Cadets, the 10-horsepower, hydrostatically driven Model 109 is as attractive as it is useful. This nicely refurbished machine is still on the job in Kansas.

company lines in April 1981. According to the serial numbers, IH manufactured approximately 693,658 regular production Cub Cadets in a 21-year span. With so many out there, IH Cub Cadets make an excellent collectible and very useable heavy-duty lawn and garden tractor.

High quality notwithstanding, IH fell into deep financial trouble by late 1980, as economic woes hit the agricultural market hard. The company ended up selling the Cub Cadet line to Modern Tool and Die Company (MTD) as the Cub Cadet Corporation (CCC) in 1981. Red 82 Series IH Cub Cadets continued to be built by CCC for delivery to IH dealers. At the same time, CCC-built yellow-and-white 82 Series tractors were sold as Cub Cadets (with no IH insignia) by lawn and garden dealers.

John Deere

Deere and Company's Models 110, 110H, 112, 112H, and 140 entered the 1970s virtually unchanged from the prior decade, but a new Model 120 was added. The 120 was essentially an entry-level hydrostatic-drive tractor patterned after the 140 but with a 12-horsepower engine. The 120 was offered in traditional John Deere colors, as well as the so-called patio colors, and it was discontinued in 1971.

By 1971, the custom patio color scheme had pretty much become only a bad memory for dealers, who were left with excess inventory like colored seats. In 1972, an upgraded version of the 110 tractor was released (alongside an eight-horsepower model with manual lift) with a 10-horsepower Kohler engine and manual or hydraulic

71

New for 1979, John Deere's Model 317 is representative of the entire 200 Series and 300 Series lineup. These machines had very modern styling, an excellent selection of engines and transmissions, and remained in production for many years.

Cub Cadet's Model 800 was an introductory model in the second-generation wide-frame lineup that was called the Quietline because it conformed to government sound regulations.

Billed as the thoroughbred of workhorses, the Allis-Chalmers Model 917 offered three PTO centers, a hydrostatic drive, and a shipping weight of more than 800 pounds.

Deere and Company's Model 112H featured a hydraulic lift that made many chores go more easily. This particular machine is routinely put through its paces at plow day and pulling events around the country.

lift. The 112 tractors received 12-horsepower engines and were consolidated into one model with an electric implement lift only. The 10-horsepower 110s received the electric lift in 1973, but the 8-horsepower 110s did not. The Models 110, 112, and 140 remained in production until late 1974, when they were replaced with the 200 and 300 Series garden tractors.

The newly designed 200 Series garden tractors were released for the 1975 model year. The new lineup included five models that were similar to their predecessors in the way implements attached, their transmissions, and the mechanically controlled PTO clutch. The Models 200, 210, 212, 214 were equipped with 8-, 10-, 12-, and 14-horsepower Kohler engines, respectively. All were equipped with Peerless four-speed transaxles and Deere's V-belt variable-speed drive/clutch system. Interestingly, all of these tractors came standard with a mechanical lift, although spring-assist attachments, electric lift, and hydraulic lift were optionally available. In 1976, the line received some relatively minor styling changes, which

included a change from screened engine compartment side panels to louvered ones. The 200 Series tractors remained in production well beyond the 1970s. They all received electromagnetic PTO clutches in 1979. That same year, the 16-horsepower Model 216 was released.

The Model 140 was replaced with the Model 300 in 1975. The 300 was equipped with a 16-horsepower Kohler engine and had beefier styling with headlights integral to the hood and a black plastic instrument panel. The Model 300 offered enhanced hydraulics. This tractor was renamed the 316 during 1978 and should not be confused with the redesigned 316 that was released in 1984.

Similar in principal to the Model 120, the Model 312 was offered in 1977 and 1978 as an entry-level hydrostatic-drive with a 12-horsepower engine. This tractor was similar to the 316, but it lacked side panels, steering brakes, and the more sophisticated hydraulics of the 316.

In 1979, the 312 and 316 were replaced with the 314 and 317, respectively. Both were hydrostatically driven, but the entry-level 314 offered only 14-horsepower in a single-cylinder Kohler powerplant, while the 317 made use of Kohler's 17-horsepower horizontally opposed twin-cylinder engine. These models remained in production into the 1980s.

With the horsepower wars alive and well in the garden tractor industry, Deere and Company entered the fray in a big way in 1975 with its largest and most powerful garden tractor to date. The Model 400 featured styling that was reminiscent of the company's larger farm tractors, and it offered a whopping 20 horsepower (Kohler engine), power steering, dual remote hydraulics, and a third circuit to operate the optional Category 0 three-point hitch. The machine also came equipped with a rear PTO and two-speed hydrostatic transmission. By many accounts, this tractor was the first of the so-called super garden tractors. The machine was replaced in the early 1980s.

Massey Ferguson

Massey Ferguson entered the 1970s with the MF 10 and MF 12 garden tractors in a lineup that included lighter and lower-powered lawn tractors. Within a few years, that lineup was expanded to include MF 14 and MF 16 models. The number designates the horsepower.

The 16-horsepower Snapper-built Massey Ferguson Model 1650 replaced the older-styled MF 16 by the end of the 1970s.

The MF 16 was powered with Kohler's 16-horsepower single-cylinder engine and featured a hydrostatic transmission. The MF 14 came equipped with a 14-horsepower Kohler and hydrostatic drive, while the MF 12 utilized Tecumseh's 27.7-cubic-inch 12-horsepower engine with hydrostatic drive in the early years and a four-speed Peerless transaxle later. The gear-driven 10-horsepower Tecumseh-powered MF 10 was really considered to be a lawn tractor at that time. These machines went out of production in 1976.

Snapper-built tractors such as the Model 1200, 1450, 1650, and others replaced the early-style Massey Ferguson garden tractors. Between then and now, Ingersoll produced Massey Ferguson garden tractors, and shortly after the company was acquired by AGCO, Simplicity built at least some of them. Today, Massey Ferguson garden tractors are manufactured by Simplicity and other members of the Briggs & Stratton Power Products Group, LLC.

Oliver

Oliver was late in its foray into the lawn and garden arena, and its tenure was brief. Jacobsen produced the company's little tractors in the early 1970s. Some records indicate that the Olivers were built from 1972 to 1974 and that most were 1972 models and were sold in 1973.

The Oliver lineup included five models—the 75 gear drive (a lawn tractor), the 105 gear drive, the 125 gear drive, the 125 hydrostatic drive, and the 145 hydrostatic. All were Kohler powered, and some bore the Cockshutt name. In either case, the tractors were essentially standard Jacobsen models with unique styling that included hoods and other body pieces. Needless to say, one of the most difficult aspects to collecting these Oliver garden tractors is that replacement body parts are very hard to find.

Case

Case entered the 1970s with four garden tractor models: the 220, 222, 442, and 444. All were equipped with the two-speed hydraulically driven transmission. The

The Oliver Model 125 hydro was really a Jacobsen in disguise. This tractor, though favored by Oliver and garden tractor collectors alike, is difficult to find body parts for since they were Oliver-specific.

Model 220, 222, 442, and 444 were powered with Kohler single-cylinder engines rated at 10-, 12-, and 14-horsepower, respectively.

The 442 (12 horsepower) and 444 (14 horsepower) were taller, wider, and longer overall compared with their 200 Series counterparts. They were also equipped with lower gearing that resulted in slightly slower ground speeds in spite of larger tires. The 442 and 444 had substantially higher ground clearance, which made them ideal for serious gardeners. The 442's last production year was 1972. It was ostensibly replaced with the 14-horsepower 224 the next year. Models 220, 222, 224, and 444 remained in production through the 1970s.

In 1972, Case added a 16-horsepower Model 446 to the lineup, along with the more versatile loader utility Models 644 and 646. The 446 Hydriv was powered with Onan's 16-horsepower engine and could be equipped with a Category 0 three-point hitch. The 644 and 646 were essentially beefed-up loader versions of the 444 and

Although it was replaced in the late 1960s, the Case Model 195 could be seen working on estates and small farms well into the 1980s.

By the end of the 1970s, Case garden tractor styling changes included new paint and decals. This Model 444 has no difficulty powering its way through tough wet snow. *Author's collection*

446. These tractors also remained in production through the decade.

In 1973, Case's Model 210 came on the scene. This tractor illustrated a major departure from the company's standard garden tractor design in that it was gear driven. The 210 was powered with a 10-horsepower Kohler engine and came standard with a belt-driven four-speed transaxle with belt-idler clutch. First gear on this tractor was actually a low-low or creeper gear perfectly suited to grading, tilling, and other slow-speed high-torque work. The 210 remained in production well into the 1980s.

Bolens

The Bolens garden tractor lineup for 1970 was somewhat abbreviated, but largely unchanged from 1969—except for the model names. The 770 manual and electric start were renamed the 730 and 733. Both were powered with seven-horsepower Briggs & Stratton engines and came with Peerless three-speed transmissions. Model 775 was renamed the 736. It was essentially a 770 with the six-

Billed as the toughest of the tough, the Model 646, one of Case's miniature loader tractors, was said to have been designed from the "rubber up" and could also be equipped with a small back hoe. *Author's collection*

speed Peerless transmission. The 850 was renamed the 853, and the new model used Briggs & Stratton power instead of a Wisconsin powerplant. The 853 came equipped with the Bolens three-speed transmission.

Model 1053 replaced the 1050. This new tractor was powered with an updated 10-horsepower Wisconsin engine and used the Bolens six-speed transmission. Also, the new Model 1253 effectively replaced the 1220 in a package that included a 12-horsepower Tecumseh powerplant (replacing the Wisconsin engine) and the six-speed Peerless drive. The Model 1256 effectively replaced the 1225 and came equipped with a 12-horsepower Wisconsin engine and Eaton hydrostatic transmission system. A 12-horsepower Tecumseh-powered version of the 1256 was also available as the 1257. The old Model 1455 became the 1457 and was equipped with a 14-horsepower Wisconsin engine and Eaton hydrostatic transmission.

In 1971, Bolens released several new small-frame tractors using a stamped-steel frame. These Models 510, 610, 613, and 813 were powered with five-, six-, six-, and eight-horsepower Briggs & Stratton engines, respectively. All utilized Peerless three-speed transaxles and today would be categorized as lawn tractors. The Models 510 and 610 had manual start. That same year, the 853 was back virtually unchanged, but the 1053 was replaced with the 1054, which was Wisconsin powered. Likewise, the 1253 was replaced with the 1254, which replaced the Tecumseh engine with a Wisconsin one. The 1256 remained in the 1971 lineup.

The most significant changes in the lineup came in the higher horsepower range. Out was the Model 1455 and in were the 14-horsepower Wisconsin-powered 1476 and 1477 and the hefty 18-horsepower Kohler-powered 1886. These big machines all utilized the Sunstrand 15U

The Bolens Model 1050 was replaced in 1970 with the Model 1053, in a package that was virtually identical to the earlier model, except for the paint job.

The Bolens Husky G14 was closely related to the 1453 that preceded it. The 14-horsepower garden tractor remained popular throughout most of the 1970s. *Author's collection*

hydrostatic drive. In 1972, a 15-horsepower Tecumseh-powered and Eaton hydro-equipped Model 1556 came on line as the 1476 and 1477 were dropped.

In 1973, Bolens introduced its G, H, and Q Series tractors. The G8 was essentially an updated Model 813, while the tube-framed G10 replaced the 1055. The G14 was basically a 1453, and the H16 was a 16-horsepower Tecumseh-powered and Eaton hydro–equipped machine. Large frame tractors for the year included the 16-horsepower Onan-equipped QT16, 18-horsepower Kohler-equipped HT18, and 19.5-horsepower Kohler-equipped HT20.

Model H16 was dropped in 1974, but a 14-horsepower Tecumseh-powered H14 was added. As the HT18 was dropped, a 16-horsepower Kohler-powered QS16 was added. The Bolens lineup for 1975 included Models G8, G10, G14, H14, QS16, QT16, and HT20.

The 1976 model year was characterized with a lineup expansion that included a few new engine/transmission combinations in machines that were well proven.

For example, a Model G9 was offered with an eight-horsepower Briggs & Stratton engine coupled to a Bolens three-speed transmission. The eight-horsepower Briggs & Stratton–powered G8 with a three-speed Peerless transmission was also in the lineup. The full model list for the year included the G8, G9, G10, G12, G14, GT14, H14, H16, QS16, QT16, and HT20. In 1977, the H14 was renamed the H14XL.

Big news for 1978 was the addition of four Iseki-built and Mitsubishi-powered diesel tractors, the G152, G154, G172, and G174. The Bolens diesels were small farm tractors and had robust hydraulics, three-point hitches, and other big-tractor features. The 15X and 17X models were equipped with 15- and 17-horsepower two-cylinder diesel engines, respectively. The XX2 and XX4 models were two-wheel drive and four-wheel drive, respectively. These little tractors really spanned the gap between the so-called super garden tractors and compact utility tractors of the day. Today, they would be classified as subcompact tractors.

In 1979, Bolens really embraced the lawn tractor versus garden tractor debate by renaming its lowest-powered small frame machines the LT8 and LT8E (with electric start). At the opposite end of the scale, four additional Iseki-built diesel models were added to the company's line, including the 19- and 24-horsepower Isuzu-powered Models G192, G194, G242, and G244. The 19X models had three speeds and three ranges for a total of nine forward gears, while the 24X models used a 3-6 configuration for a total of 18 forward gears.

Jacobsen

In 1970, Jacobsen's garden tractor lineup included the gear-driven 8- and 10-horsepower Chief 800 and Chief 1000, the hydrostatically driven 12-horsepower Super Chief 1200, and both manual lift and electric lift versions of the company's 14-horsepower hydrostatic tractor. The Chief 800 and 1000 used Kohler engines, four-speed transmissions, and belt-idler clutch and driveline arrangements. The higher-powered tractors also used Kohler engines and V-belt drives to transfer power from

Jacobsen's Super Chief 1200 Hydro was in the lineup for 1970. This tractor's styling appears in tractors wearing the Ford brand as well.

the engine to the transmission. These machines all used a single-band brake that engaged the transmission differential pinion shaft. These tractors were replaced in 1971 with a new GT series.

At the top end of the scale for 1971, Jacobsen offered the GT-14, a 14-horsepower Kohler-powered tractor with hydrostatic transmission. This robust tractor used a shaft to couple the hydro to the engine through a two-speed range box. Top speed forward was 6.5 miles per hour in high and 4.4 miles per hour in low. The 12-horsepower GT-12 hydro was similarly equipped, but it used a manual lift instead of hydraulic. The GT-12 gear-driven tractor used the same 12-horsepower Kohler engine as the GT-12 hydro, but it was coupled to a four-speed transaxle using a belt-idler clutch and driveline. This tractor could be ordered with the optional electric implement lift. The entry-level Model GT-10 was released with a 10-horsepower Kohler engine in a package that was very similar to the GT-12 gear drive.

In 1973, Jacobsen added the 16-horsepower single-cylinder Kohler-powered GT-16 to the lineup. This hydrostatically driven workhorse came standard with hydraulic lift and automotive-type worm gear steering. A three-point hitch was optional.

In 1977, Jacobsen released a newly styled lineup that included the 1000 and 1200 gear-driven tractors and the 1250, 1450, and 1650 hydros. These tractors had similar dimensions to their predecessors, and all were still Kohler powered. Both the 14- and 16-horsepower models came standard with hydraulic lift. The gear drives offered four forward speeds. These tractors remained in production through the decade.

Ford

Ford's garden tractor models for the 1970s included the 100, 120, 125, 145, 165, and 195. They all shared a 46-inch-wheelbase chassis and were powered with 10-, 12-, 14-, and 16-horsepower single-cylinder Kohler engines, respectively. Models 125, 145, and 165 were equipped

ABOVE: The Jacobsen-built Ford 165 garden tractor had a 16-horsepower engine coupled to a hydrostatic transmission. This model came standard with hydraulic lift.

RIGHT: Dual-pedal hydrostatic control is characteristic of this later 14-horsepower Ford Model 145 tractor. This machine was also a product of the Jacobsen factory.

with hydrostatic transmissions and offered hydraulic lift. Models 100 and 120 offered the four-speed Peerless Model 2306A transaxle with belt-idler clutch and a standard manual lift. The 125, 145, and 165 all used Peerless transaxles driven with Eaton hydrostatic units. Ford also had a more powerful 19.5-horsepower two-cylinder Kohler-powered Model 195 that featured hydrostatic transmission, hydraulic lift, front and rear PTO, and power steering.

Ford continued to use Jacobsen-built garden tractors through the decade.

General Electric

By the late 1960s, General Electric had completed at least three years of testing with five different garden tractor prototypes and production models. These machines were designed in response to the growing interest in alternate fuels and the impending oil crisis that seemed to loom right along with unrest in oil-producing countries. What made them stand apart in the market is that they were powered with electric motors fed with batteries rather than the more conventional engine and petroleum combination.

In 1969, the company offered three models of these for consumers: the Elec-Trak E12, E15, and E20. The tractors were all driven by electric motors coupled to Peerless 2300 Series multispeed transaxles. The E12 was initially offered to fill the 12-horsepower tractor niche. The E15 and E20 went head to head with 14- and 16-horsepower machines, respectively.

The high-end E20 was available with eight forward and four reverse speeds with automatic downshift and push-button cruise control. Not surprisingly, the implement lift was electric, as were the PTO outputs. The machine could be fit with a number of mowers, snow removal tools, tillers, and plug-in handheld tools, such as a power drill, hedge trimmer, and more. The E20 had a top speed of nine miles per hour.

In the middle of the pack, the E15 offered seven forward gears with a four-speed range box for a total of 28 forward speeds and four reverse. As with the E16, power from the electric motor was fed to the transaxle through a V-belt drive. This 850-pound workhorse achieved a seven-mile-per-hour top speed. The introductory-level E12 garden tractor offered three forward speeds with a four-speed range box, which yielded 12 forward gears and three reverse. Top speed for the E12 was about six miles per hour.

For a number of years, General Electric had built tractors for Avco New Idea and Wheel Horse, but by the mid-1970s sales were well below targets. As a result, General Electric went shopping for a buyer for its

General Electric's Elec-Trak E20 was listed in the 14- to 16-horsepower class when it was first released. This machine could be equipped with mowing decks, rotary tillers, and other implements that were powered from the tractor's battery pack.

Wheel Horse's B-145 Elec-Trak was a product of the GE plant initially, but Wheel Horse owned the entire line by the end of the 1970s.

The 18-horsepower General Electric–built EGT200 was branded by agricultural implement maker Avco New Idea, a company that's better known for harvesting equipment and manure spreaders.

This 1970s vintage Speedex Model 1030 is still on the job in central Pennsylvania. Here, its owner enjoys turning some early spring ground.

Elec-Trak division. The employees tried to purchase the line, but weren't able to do so before it was sold to Wheel Horse. On July 23, 1973, Wheel Horse announced that it was purchasing the assets of General Electric's outdoor power products division and the new owner continued to produce Elec-Trak tractors with the Wheel Horse name on them until at least the late 1970s.

Elec-Trak garden tractors are particularly collectible and useful today as the global petroleum shortage again is an issue. It seems ironic that now, almost 40 years after it first went to market, electric lawn and garden equipment is on everyone's mind.

Speedex

In 1969, under General Combustion's ownership (later merging with Mechtron International), Speedex

This original-condition Speedex Model 1430 brings nothing but smiles, with its beefy 14-horsepower engine, chain reduction drive, and a ticket to hook up to the pulling sled.

Who says you need shaft drive and an automotive-type clutch to make a good showing at the garden tractor pulls? This Speedex Model 1430 brings as much joy to its owners as it does the spectators.

production was increased to around 1,500 units a year. The company also developed a full-floating mower deck and an awesome diesel-powered tractor, the 882, during the decade.

Early 1970s Speedex models had rounded hoods and included the 400-pound, 8-horsepower S-17, the 650-pound 10-horsepower S-24, the 8-horsepower S-19 (it came standard with belly-mount rotary mower), and the 14-horsepower S-32. These tractors were for the most part Briggs & Stratton powered, and the S-32 became the All American Model 3200 in 1973. All the tractors utilized a gear transmission and belt-idler clutch and

driveline system. These tractors could be equipped with blades, mowers, and a number of ground-engaging rear-mounted attachments. Even a front-end loader was recommended for the 14-horsepower model. Shortly after their release, the tractors' hoods were made with a series of flat bends, which approximated a smooth curve.

By 1976, the Speedex lineup included the 16-horsepower Model 1632 Spirit of 76, which could be ordered with either Kohler or Briggs & Stratton power. This flagship tractor featured dual independent rear brakes. Options included a Category 0 three-point hitch, hydraulic lift, and PTO. The 1030, 1230, and 1430

This beautifully restored Sears Suburban 12 is equipped with a fully functional dump rake, which was used to windrow hay. Note the cast grille housing and attractive David Bradley styling.

Golden Eagle models were also part of the lineup. These had three-speed automotive-type transmissions, heavy-duty differential, and geared steering. The Golden Eagles were powered with 10-, 12-, or 14-horsepower engines, respectively. Speedex also offered the 11-horsepower 1130 and 1140 and the 16-horsepower 1630 high-ground-clearance tractor. These tractors had three- (1130 and 1630) and four-speed transmissions. The lineup remained virtually unchanged for the next couple of years.

In 1979, Speedex offered the 1040-A, an improved 10-horsepower model with slightly updated sheet metal and a four-speed transmission. The 1240 was a 12-horsepower version of the same tractor. At the end of the decade, the company also offered three larger 16-horsepower tractors: the entry-level 1630, 1631, and 1632. The 1631 came standard with the Category 0 three-point hitch and tri-rib front tires, and it was sold as the perfect tractor for the professional or amateur truck

farmer. The flagship 1632 was similar to the 1631, but it had additional hydraulic capability and amenities.

Speedex tractors from the 1970s are still very capable and remain highly collectible. The stout little machines look a little dated for their age because the corporate strategy was to offer a functional, long-lasting machine at a reasonable price; accordingly, there were no cigar lighters, dash panels, or beverage holders on the models.

Sears/David Bradley/Roper

In 1970, the Sears garden tractor lineup included two 12-horsepower models, the Suburban 12 and Super Suburban 12. The Super included such amenities as a cigar lighter, chrome wheel covers, and wider tires than the regular Suburban 12. Both included front and rear implement mounts and various hitches.

These machines were built by Roper and evolved slightly throughout the decade, most notably with

Power King Models 1614 and 2418 show the pinnacle of company styling through 1980. These tractors were low tech, but their well-proven designs continue to offer their owners trouble-free service. *Author's collection*

14 HP
Model 1614

4.00-12 front tires. 8.00-16 rear lawn tread tires (pictured). Also comes with 7.50-16 or 9.50-16 lug tires, or 8.30-24 lug or all-weather (diamond) tread rear tires. Has 14 hp Kohler cast-iron engine. 3 point hitch and hydraulic lift are standard.

18 HP
Model 2418

24 inch lug tread rear tires are shown with standard 4.00-12 front tires. 24" or 16" all-weather tread, or 16" lug tread rear tires are also available. Most powerful of all POWER KING models, this unit features an 18 hp Kohler cast-iron, overhead valve engine, hydraulic implement lift, and standard category "O" 3 point hitch.

increased engine power. For example, in 1971 the 14-horsepower SS14 came on line, and in 1972 the 15-horsepower SS15 (15 horsepower) became part of the lineup. In 1973, the 16-horsepower ST16 debuted. By the end of the decade, numerous ST and SS models had come and gone, along with a pair of 16-horsepower and 18-horsepower machines powered by twin-cylinder engines. By 1979, Sears offered the GT Series tractors in 16-, 18-, and 19.9-horsepower variants.

Vintage 1970s Sears lawn and garden tractors remain highly collectible today, although parts are getting more difficult to find. The more reliable Roper-built machines are now more sought after than the lighter-duty Murray-built units that first appeared (with limited models) around 1976.

Engineering Products Company

Power King and Economy tractors were both available in the 1970s. Initially, the Engineering Products Company's lineup included several Economy models, Power King models, and Jim Dandy tractors. The naming system at this time consisted primarily of a four-digit number that depicted the rear-wheel diameter and horsepower rating. These tractors were all pretty much unstyled and relied on the engine cooling ductwork to represent the front end. The machines had tinwork over the top of the engine and operator's stations with some dash sheet metal, but for the most part they were relatively bare bones in the styling department (except for the deluxe versions).

In 1974, the so-called styled tractors made it to the salesroom floor (production started in 1973). These

Wheel Horse's massive D-250 was released as a 10-speed gear-drive model in 1976. This machine is powered with a Renault water-cooled engine.

tractors remained in production until the mid-1980s. They were characterized by a vertically slotted grille and hoods that were hinged at the dash (which opened from the front). Headlights on these styled tractors were integral with the grille housing. Fourteen-horsepower tractors were introduced that same year, and even the diminutive Jim Dandy lineup included a new 14-horsepower model. The Jim Dandy line's frame also changed that year to a more modern ladder-style design.

In 1977, all the Engineering Power Company tractors came off the line wearing the Power King name. Models included the 14-horsepower gear-driven 1614 and 2414, 18-horsepower 1618 and 2418, and 16-horsepower 1616 and 2416. These tractors all sported a three-speed transmission, although a pair of them could be installed in some cases to yield an effective nine forward and three reverse gears. The 1612 also was offered near the end of the 1970s. This 12-horsepower tractor was an entry-level Jim Dandy derivative.

These tractors remained in production through the decade and remain highly collectible today.

Wheel Horse

By the end of the 1960s, Wheel Horse had diversified to the extent that it had a plant in Belgium, a joint venture with a Norwegian mower firm, and ownership

In 1974, the Model B-100 made a perfect match for ground-engaging tools like this PTO-powered rotary tiller. *Author's collection*

of several other companies. Two interesting acquisitions included Sno-Flight snowmobiles and Skystream, an aviation company. The Sno-Flight project netted the company the Wheel Horse Safari snowmobile, among others, and buying Skystream tapped Wheel Horse directly into the business aviation world.

In the early 1970s, Wheel Horse found itself in need of capital and cutting its workforce. After losing several million dollars, Cecil Pond put his company up for sale. On May 24, 1974, American Motors Corporation purchased Wheel Horse and planned to run the company as a wholly owned subsidiary.

In 1970, the company's garden tractor lineup included 7- and 8-horsepower Commando models; 7-, 8, and 12-horsepower Charger models; 10- and 12-horse-

power Raider models; the General Electric–built Electro 12; and the high-end GT-14. These models didn't change very substantially in form, function, or name for the next several years.

The 1973 Wheel Horse garden tractor lineup included the 8-horsepower four speed, 8-horsepower eight speed, 10-horsepower eight speed, 12-horsepower eight speed, 8-horsepower hydro, 14-horsepower eight speed, 14-horsepower hydro, GT-14, 16-horsepower hydro, and 18-horsepower hydro. This full range of tractors was due to change for the next year.

Wheel Horse released its letter series machines in 1974. The B Series included a nice selection of medium-duty garden tractors that offered high value in a lower price bracket. The C Series tractors were the most popular models and, in the spirit of true garden tractors, could stand up to grueling ground-engaging work. The D Series machines were akin to the super garden tractors offered by other companies. These big little machines were geared for large estate or commercial duty.

Initially, the B Series included the 8-horsepower B-80 with four-speed transmission and the 10-horsepower B-100 with hydro. The C Series included the 10-horsepower C-10 with eight-speed transmission, the 12-horsepower C-120 hydro, the C-120 eight speed, and the C-160 hydro and eight speed. The heavier-duty D Series included Models D-160 hydro, D-180 hydro, and D-200 hydro. The following year, an Elec-Trak Model B-145 joined the stable along with an electric B-185.

In 1976, Wheel Horse's garden tractor lineup included the B-60, B-80, and B-100 eight-speed tractors with 6, 8, and 10 horsepower, respectively. The B-145 Elec-Trak was also launched that year, along with eight-speed and hydro C-120 models, eight-speed and hydro C-160 models, and the C-185 Elec-Trak. D Series 1976 models included the D-160 and D-200 hydros and a D-250 with 10-speed transmission. For 1977, the company's garden tractors were virtually unchanged.

Wheel Horse's models for 1978 included the B-81 with a four-speed transmission, the B-111 four speed, the C-81 eight speed, the C-101 eight speed, the C-121 with eight speeds or hydro, the C-141 with eight speeds or hydro, the C-161 with eight speeds or hydro, the C-161 Twin with eight speeds or hydro, the D-160 hydro, the D-200 hydro, and the D-250 with a 10-speed transmission.

In the last year of the decade, Wheel Horse's garden tractor lineup included three B Series tractors. At the low end of the power scale, the eight-horsepower B-81 offered a six-speed transmission, while the B-111 could be purchased with either a six-speed or four-speed transmission. The well-rounded C Series included the C-81 eight speed, the C-101 eight speed, the C-111 eight speed, the C-121 eight speed or hydro, the C-141 eight speed or hydro, the C-161 eight speed or hydro, and the C-161 Twin eight speed or hydro. The D-160 and D-200 hydros also were available, as was the D-250 with 10-speed transmission.

Tractors very similar to the 1979 lineup were available into the 1980s.

Gravely

In many respects, Gravely still owned the two-wheeled garden tractor market by the 1970s. The company had arguably the most robust transmission system and a unique set of PTO-driven attachments that made the tractors some of the most versatile available at any time. Several so-called convertible models could be equipped with a sophisticated sulky to make them riders.

The company entered the four-wheel riding tractor market in 1967 with the Models 424, 430, and 432. Shortly later, a Model 450 joined the lineup. These machines were produced through 1970, and all featured a rear engine mounted directly to an all-gear planetary transmission. The transmission was adapted from the walk-behind models and had the Swiftamatic two-speed differential. Early Model 424 and 430 tractors were powered with 10-horsepower or 12-horsepower engines, respectively, which were built by either Onan or Kohler. Later, only the Kohler engine was offered. The 432 was powered with a 14-horsepower Kohler, and the 450 used a 16.5-horsepower Onan engine. These garden tractors had either four- or eight-speed shuttle-type transaxles. They could be equipped with front- and mid-mount PTO-driven equipment and were fully capable of pulling ground-engaging trailing equipment.

In 1970, these early Gravely garden tractors were retired and replaced with the 800 Series tractors. These new rear-engine machines ranged in power from the 10 horsepower to 16.5 horsepower range and utilized a new eight-speed shuttle transmission that was designed specifically for the four-wheel tractors. Models 800, 812, and 814 were powered with 10-horsepower, 12-horsepower, and 14-horsepower Kohler single-cylinder engines, respectively. The Model 816 used the 16.5-horsepower twin-cylinder Onan. The 800 Series tractors offered PTO power at the front, mid, and rear, with a hydraulic lift standard on the 816. Models 812 and 814 could be ordered with hydraulics from the factory for an additional cost. The 810 offered only manual lift. The 800 Series tractors were replaced in 1978 with the 8000 Series.

The 10-horsepower Model 8102 replaced the earlier Model 810. Models 8122 and 8123 (Models 8126 and 8127 were the commercial versions) were virtually identical to the 812 and featured Gravely's eight-speed transaxle and 12-horsepower Kohler power. The 8122 offered manual lift, and the 8123 was equipped with hydraulics. The 8162 and 8163 used a 16-horsepower twin-cylinder Onan engine for power; the 8163 had hydraulic lift. Models 8166 and 8167 used a 16-horsepower Briggs & Stratton engine, while the 8177 came equipped with Onan's 16.5-horsepower engine. Gravely's Model 8183 had an 18-horsepower twin-cylinder Onan. Models 8179 and 8199 came with twin-cylinder Onan engines rated at 16.5 and 18 horsepower, respectively. The 8000 Series tractors remained in the lineup well into the 1980s.

Simplicity

The Simplicity lineup for 1970 included the 3310V and 3310H Landlord models and the 3314V and 3314H Sovereigns. The Landlord tractors were powered with 10-horsepower Briggs & Stratton engines and could be equipped with a three-speed transaxle and variable-speed belt drive. The 3310 offered hydrostatic drive. The higher-end Sovereigns utilized 12-horsepower Briggs & Stratton engines. All models shared a frame and sheet metal. These tractors were somewhat retro in their styling compared with many other garden tractors of the time; for example, their headlights were mounted on stalks bolted to the sides of the grille housing.

For the 1971 model year, the Landlords and Sovereigns were redesigned with new body panels, grille, and more. Headlights on these tractors were still mounted on the sides of the grille housing, but they were more modern looking and were partially enclosed. Both tractor series came with either variable-speed or hydrostatic drive. The Sovereign was now equipped with a 14-horsepower engine and electric implement lift.

By mid-1972, Simplicity offered a 15-horsepower Briggs & Stratton–powered set of Sovereign tractors. The

Model 3415S utilized a new four-speed forward and four-speed reverse shuttle transmission, while the 3415H featured hydrostatic drive. The Landlord was available in three configurations, all with 10-horsepower engines. The 3410 used a three-speed sliding spur-gear transmission; the 3410S was equipped with the four-speed shuttle; and the 3410H had a hydrostatic transmission. The three-speed variable-drive system was no longer used on either the Sovereign or Landlord line.

In 1973, the Sovereign was upgraded with a 16-horsepower Briggs & Stratton powerplant and a choice of hydrostatic drive (on the Model 3416H) or the four-speed forward and reverse shuttle transmission (Model 3416S). That same year, the 10-horsepower Briggs & Stratton Landlord could be equipped with the relatively new shuttle transmission (the Model 3410S) or straight three-speed gear drive (the Model 3410).

Simplicity also released the large-framed Model 4014 in 1973. This machine was designed to fill the niche between garden tractors and utility tractors. It was one of the first so-called super garden tractors. The Model 4014 was powered with Onan's 19.5-horsepower twin-cylinder engine, and the tractor came standard with three PTOs and could be fit with the optional Category 0 three-point hitch. The tractor was innovative in the market for many reasons, not the least of which was that it had both a hydrostatic speed transmission and a three-speed sliding spur-gear range box. When the machine was released, so was an entire set of attachments that were ready to take advantage of its increased capacity and size.

By mid-decade, the 4000 Series machines had been replaced with 7000 Series tractors, including the 7010 and 7013 Landlords and the 7016 Sovereign. These machines offered 10, 13, and 16 horsepower in a package that was essentially identical to their predecessors. Additionally, the 4014 was renamed the 9020.

In 1978, redesigned Landlord Models 7010 and 7012 were released with Kohler engines, as was a 14-horsepower Briggs & Stratton–powered 7014. The Model 7010 was equipped with a six-speed transmission, Model 7012 offered a hydrostatic drive, and the 7014 was equipped

Simplicity's 15-horsepower Sovereign (bottom) and 10-horsepower Landlord garden tractors made a formidable pair. The former came with a Vickers piston-to-piston hydrostatic drive (three gear ranges), which was optional on the lower-powered model.

with a four-speed semi-automatic. All of these tractors now had their headlights integrated into the top of the grille.

Three Sovereign models also were available in 1978. At the high end of the scale was the 18-horsepower Kohler-powered Model 7018 Hydro accompanied by the 16-horsepower Kohler-powered Model 7016 Hydro. A six-speed gear-driven Sovereign Model 7016 was offered as well.

At the larger end of the size and power scale, the 19.5-horsepower Onan-powered 9020 Powermax was back, looking pretty much as it did in its earlier iteration. The company also offered a pair of more capable diesel-powered machines, the 9528 (with 28 horsepower) and the 9523 (with 23 horsepower). These latter two tractors were marketed to small farmers, commercial businesses, large estate owners, park districts, and the like. They were far more tractor than most homeowners really needed.

BRINLY-HARDY

Brinly's Gard-N-Cart was part grille guard and part cargo platform (when folded down). The attachment was available to fit a number of garden tractor brands and remains so popular today that several folks are fabricating replicas.

When John Brinly set up his Simpsonville, Kentucky, blacksmith shop around 1800, he couldn't possibly have imagined that his legacy would include some of the hottest garden tractor collectibles out there in the twenty-first century. Nor could his son Thomas E. C. Brinly have imagined that the steel plow he fashioned from an old saw blade in 1837 would set the stage for a 165-year-long plow-making run that is still going on. Most certainly neither of them could have imagined a business in 2008 devoted almost exclusively to building implements and attachments designed for the suburban homeowner's lawn and garden; however, that's exactly what the still-privately-held Brinly-Hardy Company excels at today.

According to retired Brinly-Hardy Vice President of Engineering Bill Doering, the company first became interested in making attachments for garden tractors in the mid- to late 1940s. "[Company leaders] wanted to find a use for their product line of mule- or horse-drawn small garden plows, cul-

tivators, and the like," Doering said. "They also had a line of larger tools for smaller tractors such as the Ferguson at that time." Although Brinly-Hardy is best known today for its big lineup of consumer-oriented tools, these have been the company's principal focus only for the past 20 years.

Brinly's lineup of modern-day garden tillage implements traces its roots (and in some cases the model numbers) back to the early 1960s when Bill Doering was first hired as chief engineer. Also, it's the company's interesting array of attachments (some quite short-lived) from those years that really captivate collectors today. "We weren't in the business of creating collectibles," Bill Doering said. "We wanted to help people get the most they possibly could out of their garden tractors." Bill and his group applied a great deal of innovation and creativity to that end, and like many engineering teams of yesterday they inadvertently produced a number of pieces that are prized today.

Setting the Standard

As a company devoted to making garden tractors more useful, Brinly-Hardy was focused on a niche that the tractor manufacturers appreciated, especially since production numbers for specialized implements were often quite low. Sometimes, of course, low production numbers translate to low profit or, worse, high costs associated with an implement's development. Brinly's solution to this problem was to make common attachments that could fit on all brands of garden tractors, but the company's early efforts were frustrated by variations in hitches.

"We could use standard parts at the working end of the attachments, but we had to accommodate all of the different hitches," Doering said. "As an implement manufacturer, our goal was to benefit owners, tractor manufacturers, and ourselves by developing hitch and drawbar standards for garden tractors."

In the early 1960s, Doering's engineering team put together a proposal for the first universal lawn and garden tractor standards by submitting drawings and measurements

Far and away the most popular (and still available new) sleeve-hitch attachment that Brinly made is the single-bottom plow. It was the company's push to standardize garden tractor hitches that made it possible.

to the appropriate American Society of Agricultural Engineers (ASAE) committees, which were made up of the tractor manufacturer's representatives. After only minor changes, standards for the drawbar, tubular sleeve hitch, and Category 0 three-point hitches were adopted for lawn and garden tractors. "Once the standards were accepted, we could standardize our implements," Doering said, "and then we started making hitches for some manufacturers OEM."

Hitches weren't the only garden tractor parts that Brinly-Hardy manufactured on an OEM basis. The company also produced rotary tillers, tiller tines, and other tools for John Deere, Elec-Trak, Ariens, Massey Ferguson, and others.

Interesting Attachments

Garden tractor enthusiasts collect Brinly-Hardy implements for a number of reasons, but one of the most compelling is to get more "seat time" doing productive work with their favorite little machines. Among many fairly traditional garden tractor attachments, Brinly-Hardy moldboard plows continue to draw lots of collector interest. In fact, the little soil-turners are so popular that many garden tractor plow events are organized each year just so that owners of vintage tractors and plows can give them both a workout. At the larger of these events, it isn't unusual to have more than 100 garden tractors turn up to 40 acres of ground in a single day.

Brinly used to make these plows with 8- and 10-inch shares, in addition to the 12-inch size that remains available today. Collectors particularly seek plows in the smaller sizes because they are relatively rare, especially those with white-painted beams and intact decals.

Brinly-Hardy's other soil-working tools—such as discs, cultivators, and spike-tooth harrows—are also favored among collectors because of their utility in the garden and because they demonstrate that vintage garden tractors were built for

Although it wasn't likely to ever be delivered with green paint on it, the Brinly single-row cultivator comes in pretty handy for weed control, at least when the crops aren't too tall.

heavy-duty ground engaging—just like a farm tractor. Also, the discs can be single- or double-gang models and the cultivators can be equipped with spikes, shovels, or spring shanks. With this variation in seedbed preparation implements alone, virtually any collector would be intrigued. As with the plows, the older-model harrows and cultivators with white-painted toolbars and frames are more desirable.

Among the most highly sought attachments to bear the Brinly name is the Model KK-100 vegetable planter, and ironically, Brinley didn't build it. "The planter was built to our specification by Cole Manufacturing Company," Doering said. Unfortunately, the sales volume was too low to offer it for many years, part of the reason it is so collectible today. The vegetable planters are also hard to find intact because the sheet metal often rusted when it came in contact with the corrosive salts in fertilizer and/or rodent waste. Even when a collector finds a relatively complete planter, it rarely has more

than a single seed plate with it. Although some folks continue to plant their gardens with the Brinly planter, most consider them to be too valuable to use.

Shifting the Weight

Another pair of unusual and highly sought-after Brinly garden tractor attachments was creatively inspired by the need for temporary forward or rearward ballast when a garden tractor was used with heavy front- or rear-mounted implements. The BB-100 Dump-Cart attachment, which consisted of a small stamped-steel wheelbarrow pan bolted to a hinged plate that pinned to the tractor's rear sleeve hitch, wasn't designed principally as a carrier. "We were making snow blades for most brands of garden tractors in the early 1960s," Doering said. "The Dump-Cart was designed to hold bags of sand or salt to help with traction." Unlike a dedicated weight box, however, the Dump-Cart also converted the tractor into a 150-

Brinly's Dump Cart wasn't really a cart at all, since it hangs from the tractor's hitch. The loaded cart could be dumped easily by pulling the catch lever.

This Cole Manufacturing single-row planter was built to Brinly's specs and sold as a Brinly planter. If you do a lot of direct seeding into the garden, this little attachment turns drudgery into fun.

pound-capacity wheelbarrow for general material handling when a heavy front implement wasn't mounted—and it was easily removed from the tractor by pulling a single pin.

In addition to heavy front blades, Brinly produced some weighty rear attachments that had a tendency to make the tractor's front end come off the ground. Brinly's solution was the Model LL-200 Gard-N-Cart. This unique attachment looks like a heavy-duty grille guard when in the raised position, and when lowered to horizontal, it makes a perfect perch for bales of peat or bags of fertilizer. So even as a gardener worked the ground with a Brinly engine-powered tiller on the rear hitch, soil amendments carried up front helped keep the tractor properly balanced. When the extra front ballast wasn't needed, the Gard-N-Cart was still a convenient platform carrier for lighter loads. Also, there's little doubt it saved many grilles from damage.

There's Still More

The wide diversity of Brinley products makes collecting the company's garden tractor attachments fun and challenging. A particularly flexible piece was the 60-inch-wide TT-100 Tool Bar, which provided the framework and hitch for connecting any manner of implement to the garden tractor. In addition,

Brinly offered several kits specifically designed to make the Tool Bar more useful. In one early 1960s catalog, kits were available for a cultivator, scarifier, scraper, disc, scratcher, and pulverizer-packer. No doubt the TT-100 also inspired many gardeners to fabricate custom attachments to suite their particular needs.

Other hard-to-find Brinly-Hardy attachments include the Rol-Aerator, the Model SS-100 Rolling Spike Harrow, and the Model RR-100 Rotary Leaf and Grass Rake, among many others. And as if that weren't enough, the company also produced rear-mounted transplanter attachments, broadcast seeders, spike aerators, turf thatchers, sweeper compactors, rollers, drag harrows, rear-mount box scrapers, rear-mount angle graders, pull-type spreaders, carts, and more. Indeed, the number of lawn and garden implements the company has produced in the past 50 years is enough to keep any collector very busy.

Under Toro's ownership, the 400 Series Wheel Horse tractors continued to be equipped with the company's proprietary Uni-Drive transaxle. *Author's collection*

CHAPTER
5

CONSOLIDATION INTO THE FUTURE
(1980 TO PRESENT)

By the mid-1970s, the value of the U.S. dollar had seriously eroded, which cost American equipment manufacturers significantly. By the decade's end, however, many companies experienced some of their most profitable years ever, but that was overshadowed by record interest rates that climbed to more than 20 percent. By 1979, the U.S. economy was in a recession that precipitously curtailed spending for the next several years.

The U.S. lawn and garden industry was hit hard, which caused serious production curtailments, several consolidations, and some outright failures. By 1980, the world was thrown into a serious recession, and some sectors of the equipment industry saw orders fall by well over 50 percent in one year. One company's losses often led to another's gains, and some emerged from the 1980s stronger.

Allis-Chalmers

In 1980, the Allis-Chalmers garden tractor lineup included the 10-, 12-, 14-, 16-, and 17-horsepower 900 Series machines listed for 1979. These tractors offered a number of features, including turf or bar-lug tires, six-speed gear-drive transmissions, shuttle transmissions, and hydrostatic transmissions. Some of the hydros also were equipped with hydraulic lift. The entry-level Model 910

was dropped for 1981, while most of the other models remained until at least the mid-1980s. New for 1980 was the 19-horsepower hydrostatically driven Model 919H and Model 920 hydrostatically driven diesel (with a Briggs & Stratton Lombardini air-cooled engine).

The 800 Series tractors in the lineup for 1980 included the 18-horsepower 818GT, as well as the models listed for 1979. These tractors were updated in 1981 for the 1982 model year to include the T-811, an 11-horsepower Briggs & Stratton–powered tractor with Vari-Shift drive coupled to a three-speed transmission; the 16-horsepower Briggs & Stratton twin-cylinder-powered Model T-816 with Vari-Drive; and the 18-horsepower twin-cylinder Model T-818. These tractors remained in the Allis-Chalmers lawn and garden lineup for several years.

In 1984, Allis-Chalmers sold the bulk of its tractor businesses to the German equipment manufacturer Deutz Corporation. That company's colors were lime green, and tractors resulting from the merger wore Deutz-Allis nameplates and were painted green. The 800 and 900 Series garden tractors were still in the lineup.

By 1987, the lime-green garden tractor list included the Briggs & Stratton twin-cylinder-powered 16-horsepower T-816 and a 12.5-horsepower T-813. Both

The Allis-Chalmers Model 914 Hydro was a large-framed machine with hydraulic lift. It came standard with traction control and a limited slip differential. Speed and direction were controlled with a single lever.

tractors had vertically oriented engines and triple-range drivetrains with Vari-Drive. Four members of the 900 Series lineup also remained that year. These included the Briggs & Stratton Lombardini diesel-powered 920D and the 12-, 14-, and 16-horsepower Kohler-powered 912H, 914H, and 916H. All of these tractors had hydrostatic transmissions and their engines were horizontally oriented. They were not only larger, but they were more robust than the 800 Series units.

The Ultima line of super garden tractors filled the agricultural/industrial/estate niche much like the earlier 718 and 720. The 1918 and 1920 both employed robust Kohler Magnum gasoline engines, hydrostatic transmissions, and a massive transaxle that included automotive-style expanding shoe drum brakes. Each was individually activated on the rear axle. Hydraulic lift was standard. Power steering was standard on the 1920, but optional on the 1918.

These Simplicity-built garden tractors remained in the Deutz-Allis lineup beyond the end of the 1980s. In 1991, AGCO (named for Allis and Gleaner) formed to purchase Deutz-Allis. Shortly thereafter, the color scheme for farm tractors, as well as lawn and garden equipment, returned to the more familiar Allis-Chalmers orange. Contrary to popular belief, White lawn and garden equipment was never related to Allis-Chalmers or Simplicity.

The 919 Hydro featured a 19-horsepower twin-cylinder Kohler engine, hydrostatic drive, and hydraulic implement lift, all of which added up to smooth efficiency and dependable service. *Author's collection*

The T-816 was a gear-drive small-framed tractor that was still capable of ground-engaging work such as plowing. The Briggs & Stratton–powered machine had a belt-idler-type clutch. *Author's collection*

MTD Corporation purchased White's outdoor power equipment before AGCO acquired the White brand.

AGCO lawn and garden equipment is still manufactured by Simplicity and other members of the Briggs & Stratton Power Products Group, LLC.

International Harvester

In the spring of 1977, IH's Outdoor Power Products Group (OPP) was given the assignment of analyzing the Cub Cadet business and making recommendations on how it should be structured in the future. At that point, IH was still first in the garden tractor arena, and the company had seen significant growth in Cadet equipment sales because of a growing number of OPP dealers that had been set up in suburban areas. Cadet sales through agricultural equipment or industrial equipment dealers, however, were static at best.

According to Harold Schramm, who was then responsible for OPP, the largest sales regions at the time for Cub Cadet were in Columbus, Ohio, and Albany, New York. He also said OPP carried a disproportionately large share of regional distribution and manufacturing expenses compared with the agricultural lines that shared

In the 1980s, Kubota became a formidable competitor in the lawn and garden tractor arena. The company offered several durable diesel-powered models, many of which are still on the job.

those plants and regions. It was clear to everyone except top management that the future of Cub Cadet and the OPP was not in the rural areas traditionally served by IH agricultural dealers, and if it were to thrive, OPP

MTD: Modern Tool and Die

Modern Tool and Die (MTD) began in 1932 as a partnership among Theo Moll, Emil Jochum, and Erwin Gerhard. The three entrepreneurs purchased both the assets and goodwill of the Modern Tool and Die Company of Cleveland, Ohio, and were quickly in the business of making tools, dies, and stampings. From an initial capital investment of $4,500, the company's first-year sales figure was about $25,000.

In 1935, MTD signed a contract with the Ergy Register Company for tooling, stampings, and completed recording registers, and by 1936 the company's first automotive stampings were produced as grilles for Graham Paige. Later, MTD produced heater cores, fenders, and other components for several manufacturers. During World War II, the company shifted focus to manufacturing components to support the defense effort, including the very recognizable mess kits issued to every soldier. MTD also did tool and die work for Goodyear and other strategic companies.

After the war, the company went back to producing automotive stampings. In 1952, MTD purchased controlling interest in Midwest Industries and expanded its manufacturing capabilities to include pedal bicycles, velocipedes, stamped-metal sandboxes, pedal cars, tricycles, and wagons. The factory, which moved to Willard, Ohio, in 1953, also began producing lawn and garden equipment in the early 1950s. In 1954, the company supplied wheelbarrows with stamped-metal pans to Sears, Roebuck and Company and offered new items such as fender skirts and bumper guards to the automotive industry.

By 1958, MTD had produced its first gasoline-engine-powered rotary mower for the fledgling lawn and garden power equipment industry. The first machine had an 18-inch cut, but 19-inch and 21-inch models quickly followed. These products were marketed through Western Auto, Montgomery Wards, B. F. Goodrich, and Firestone Tire and Rubber Company. From the very beginning, MTD opened the market for any number of consumer supply houses, building machines bearing many names other than MTD.

In 1959, MTD added a riding mower to its outdoor power products line. At that time, more than 300 companies were in the business of assembling rotary mowers, but MTD had the great advantage of producing its own stampings, giving them some control over parts supply and allowing them to customize for their individual customers. A four-horsepower engine powered the company's first riding mower, and it had a single forward and reverse speed. The 24-inch single cutting blade was directly coupled to the engine and could not be shut off.

During the next 20 years, MTD continued to carefully expand. In 1960, the company built a new manufacturing facility in Indianola, Mississippi. In 1961, MTD purchased Sehl Manufacturing Ltd., giving it a manufacturing presence in Canada with a gateway to other countries. The company's Valley City, Ohio, facility opened in 1966 and has been expanded over the years to a major campus with corporate offices, design, engineering, and call-center functions all at the location. In 1967, MTD purchased Columbia Manufacturing Company of Westfield, Massachusetts—the oldest bicycle manufacturer in the United States. In 1968, the company produced its first snow thrower, and in 1975, MTD purchased the assets of Yardman Company. It has been collecting lawn and garden equipment brands ever since.

According to Herb Hampson, retired Cub Cadet Corporation director of sales and marketing (and 20-year veteran of MTD by 1981), MTD expanded its lawn and garden manufacturing presence through the late 1970s until it was the largest in the industry. The company still lacked the brand recognition associated with IH's Cub Cadet, however, and the MTD name was most closely associated with large retailers of consumer-grade equipment (even though it offered a premium line in the Yardman brand). By 1980, therefore, the company was interested in purchasing available premium lawn and garden tractor lines. MTD's timing was perfect because many lawn and garden tractor manufacturers were struggling at the time, and MTD had production capacity to fill in its new Brownsville, Tennessee, plant.

Two years earlier, in 1978, MTD had embarked on a project that resulted in the planning for and eventual construction of a new state-of-the-art plant. The company was in a powerful growth phase, and with the strong economy, it made sense for MTD to seek out attractive locations as part of its expansion plan. Legal documents show that MTD was in negotiations with Haywood County, Tennessee, and the Industrial Development Board of the City of Brownsville to secure development bonds for the project in 1978. The Brownsville plant would be a 160,000-square-foot manufacturing facility and office space with appropriate cranes, 600-ton press, 15 punch presses, resistance welders, and other related manufacturing machinery.

According to International Harvester, MTD's new Brownsville plant was dedicated in May 1980, one full year before the formation of the Cub Cadet Corporation. In the same document, IH explains that MTD had been manufacturing outdoor power products in that plant on a private label basis, and that the plant would be solely dedicated to Cub Cadet Corporation's production after June 1, 1981.

Today, MTD produces outdoor power equipment for not only Cub Cadet, but also Troy-Bilt, White, Bolens, Yardman, and many other brands.

The Kohler Magnum–powered Deutz-Allis Ultima 1918 featured a heavy-duty differential and axle, complete with cast-iron housing. Unlike its bigger brother, the 1920, the 1918 did not come with the two-speed version of final drive. *Author's collection*

needed to become separate from and independent of the agricultural division's sales, distribution, and manufacturing organizations.

As early as 1975, Schramm was asked to find a new manufacturing facility for Cub Cadets, but the project was later killed. "I had found a totally suitable location and plant for a great price, but it was killed for political reasons," he said. In 1977, the OPP study recommended that the group find a new and separate manufacturing facility, and it even had the approval of the manufacturing member of the group (who was then assistant plant manager at Louisville). The report further recommended that the Cub Cadet line be focused on the burgeoning suburban markets, while still allowing rural markets to be served by the dwindling number of ag division dealers.

Through a seemingly impossible set of circumstances, the OPP never really had the chance to vet its proposal because of multilevel changes in management. These occurred when Ben H. Warren was appointed president of the Agricultural Equipment Division. "It was not certain what would happen to the OPP proposal since this happened before we had a chance to present it to the

Divisional Product Group," Schramm said. He eventually did meet with the new president and finance manager, however, and shortly afterward he was called back to meet with the president alone. The discussion at this meeting answered several questions related to the Cub Cadet line.

"[Ben Warren] proceeded to tell me that, in his opinion, we needed to paint the Cub Cadets red and go back to selling them through ag dealers exclusively—the ones who had put us in the business," Schramm said. "I pointed out the significant market changes and the strong brand identity with the yellow and white colors, but I was dismissed with no comment."

Schramm later shared that discussion with the OPP marketing manager, who agreed that Warren's plan would hurt Cub Cadet significantly. At that meeting, Schramm predicted that IH would be out of the Cub Cadet business within five years. On August 22, 1977, he received word that an accountant with no OPP or other direct product experience was replacing him. He transferred to other areas within the organization and was later involved with the Cub Cadet's transfer of ownership.

IH's new 82 Series tractors were released about two years later. They were painted red; and built at Louisville; they were marketed through the agricultural dealer network and existing OPP dealers. It is not clear what upper management had in store for OPP and the Cub at that time.

Cub Cadet Corporation

By 1980, the economic writing was on the wall; orders for durable goods were declining, and demand for farm, and lawn and garden equipment was cascading. MTD had built a new state-of-the-art plant, which only added to its now-excess capacity. International Harvester, faced with an almost incomprehensible debt load, was looking to shed components and get rid of floor-plan credit commitments in an attempt to generate some capital.

As a result, the Cub Cadet Corporation (CCC) was incorporated on June 1, 1981, as a wholly owned subsidiary of MTD. With that incorporation came the passing of the long and proud Cub Cadet tradition from

One of the first real changes that Cub Cadet Corporation made to IH's former lineup was to put a small Kubota diesel engine in some of the tractors. This prototype machine was eventually labeled the **882** in its first iteration. *Author's collection*

an ailing International Harvester to a vibrant, highly successful lawn and garden equipment company. Cub Cadet had come a long way under the highly stratified control structure at IH, but it would eventually blossom as a small, independent upstart known as CCC.

The specific details surrounding the formation of the Cub Cadet Corporation are not entirely clear. Since MTD was then, and continues to be, a privately held company, relatively little information has become public over the years. So just who made the initial contact is unknown. According to Herb Hampson, John McFadden (then-president of MTD) and Edward Stell (then-CEO of MTD) negotiated the purchase. Robert L. Lee, IH's general manager for OPP, announced the deal to dealers in a letter dated February 16, 1981, so the negotiation was likely initiated in 1980.

Lee's letter noted that Cub Cadet Corporation represented a new manufacturing, marketing, and distribution structure for IH's outdoor power products, and he assured dealers that the Brownsville, Tennessee, plant was one of the most modern in the industry. The letter also noted that CCC would be entirely self-funded and

The Cub Cadet Corporation built this mid-1980s Cub Cadet Model 682 for International Harvester. The tractor had a 17-horsepower Kohler engine, a Sunstrand hydrostatic transmission, and a mechanical lift.

that June 1, 1981, would be the actual date that the new corporation was to come on line.

A colorful brochure entitled *A Star Is Born* accompanied Lee's letter and further spelled out the details. The brochure noted, for example, that IH's production of the Cub Cadet had been ramped up to maximum capacity in November 1980 and would remain that way until April 1981 to cover orders and parts during the transition, which lasted longer than the three months indicated in the marketing piece. The brochure also indicated that MTD was the parent company of CCC, which provided financial stability among several other benefits. According to Hampson, CCC was actually the sales and service organization of the new venture, although the Brownsville plant was totally dedicated to the pro-

duction of Cub Cadets. And while MTD owned CCC outright, the parent company left the fledgling corporation pretty much alone.

By 1981, IH had set up a special sales organization for dealers that sold only the OPP line (a recommendation made by Harold Schramm many years earlier), and unfortunately, these dealers were out of a job once the sale was completed. As director of sales and marketing for CCC, Hampson interviewed most of those individuals, and many of them were hired into the new corporation. He notes that some territory changes were made, but he tried to keep successful people in their same general territory.

"Our first sales priority was to have the independent dealers sign a new sales agreement with CCC, and rumors

The first diesel model Cub Cadet to be sold as an IH unit was named the 782D. This tractor is virtually identical to the 882, except for the paint job.

were in the field that Cub Cadets would be sold in discount stores such as K-Mart," Hampson said. "Although many of MTD's customers, such as Montgomery Wards and Ace Hardware, wanted to handle the Cub Cadet, we refused." This policy continued until recently, when at least some lawn tractor models became available through chains such as Lowe's and Tractor Supply.

For IH agricultural equipment dealers who also sold Cub Cadets, the CCC had a different arrangement. CCC would sell tractors and equipment directly to IH, which handled pricing and distribution to dealers. Cub Cadets built for IH were to be painted red, while the others were to be painted yellow and white. "I handled the sales with IH," Hampson said. "We kept them on a very short leash on their credit line. We would ship a load directly to an IH dealer and bill IH. Our corporate credit manager didn't get much sleep in those days."

As history made very clear, IH remained in serious financial difficulty in the first several years after the Cub Cadet sale. "Later, IH wanted to sell us the [Cub] transmission line that was in Louisville," Hampson said. "The transmission was excellent, but the manufacturing procedure was outdated. At a meeting in Racine, John McFadden and I told them that we were not interested in purchasing the old transmission line, which they had planned to sell to us for one million dollars; there were a lot of jaws hitting the table when we broke the news to them." What the IH group didn't know is that CCC had already designed a new transmission that was ready for production

Once IH's Cub Cadet production was shut down at Louisville in April 1981, CCC moved all of the tooling to the Brownsville plant. "We sent our crew to the IH factory and shipped over a hundred semi loads of tooling,

Cub Cadet's 1572 super garden tractor traces its roots to IH's 982 super garden tractor. This large-frame machine also sports a Kubota diesel engine.

dies, fixtures, and parts in process," Hampson said about the magnitude of the task. "We spent much of the next year setting things up." By the time it was all over, nearly two hundred semi loads of materials had been shipped to Brownsville from IH's Louisville and Memphis facilities.

According to a CCC press release dated September 11, 1981, Hampson introduced the new company's 1982 line at the Garden Industry of America Show in Pittsburgh, even though it was not yet able to produce all of the models. The first tractor off the assembly line at Brownsville was a yellow-and-white Model 482 manufactured in late 1981. "The 482 was not a real Cub Cadet since it had a Briggs & Stratton engine and a four-speed Peerless transaxle, but it demonstrated that the plant was up and running," Hampson said. International Harvester's brochure to dealers indicated

that CCC would be in production by August 1981, but that was off by several months. The plant didn't get up to speed until well into 1982. Parts distribution was initially handled through IH's parts system, and as IH-produced parts supplies dwindled, CCC-produced parts took their place.

"Initially, IH continued to manufacture the unique rear axle [transmission and differential] for us," Hampson said. Nonetheless, CCC immediately commissioned MTD's engineering department to design new rear castings for both the hydrostatic transmission's final drive and the three-speed sliding gear transmission and differential. "Our design utilized an aluminum housing with cast-iron horns and retained the steel gears initially," Hampson said. One of the principal motivations for going to an aluminum housing was that iron foundries

The Model 1860 was built in 1990 and 1991. Note the change from tin to composite material for the hood, grille, and engine side panels. Placing the lights behind the single top lens earned these machines the nickname "Cyclops."

had found themselves squarely in the EPA's crosshairs because of major pollution issues; cost was also a factor.

In 1982, Cub Cadet products were available, but for much of the year, it was a matter of selling stock that was produced early in 1981 by IH. Some of the machines were even repainted yellow and white for marketing purposes. Late in the year, CCC's full Cub Cadet line became available. The catalog that the company produced for 1982 was also representative of the 1983 model year because the changes from 1982 to 1983 were so small.

Yellow-and-white painted Cub Cadets destined for the former OPP dealers sported a new CCC logo on the grille and behind the seat in 1982. Hydrostatic models included the 680 (same as the red 1282), 682, 782, 784 (Model 782 with front hydraulic outlets), 982, 984 (Model 982 with rear PTO), and 986 (Model 982 with

In the early twenty-first century, Cub Cadet's 3000 Series garden tractors included state-of-the-art engines, mower deck technology, and hydrostatic transmissions. Plus, they were still capable of pulling a plow.

It's not unusual for garden tractor enthusiasts to gather several times a year to work their little machines. This plow day was populated with at least 100 Cub Cadets, as well as other brands, and they turned about 20 acres of ground in a few hours.

rear PTO and front hydraulic outlets). The gear-drive tractors were virtually identical to those sold through IH dealers and included the Model 482, 580 (same as the red 582S), and 582. The Cub Cadet models destined for IH's agricultural dealers remained unchanged from 1982 to 1983, except that a new 12-horsepower hydrostatic Model 1282 was added.

The Brownsville plant built both the red-colored and yellow-and-white-colored tractors on the same assembly lines since the tractors were identical except in model numbers and color. International Harvester had wanted CCC to paint front axles, pedestals, and transmission housings red, but CCC insisted that all of the chassis components be one color (black) for manufacturing

efficiency. Not all CCC-built red Cub Cadets have the black undercarriage, though, as early pieces made use of parts obtained from IH.

Cub Cadet Corporation's first significant public event was the Garden Industry of America (GIA) show held in Pittsburgh, Pennsylvania, in the spring of 1983. At that point, the Brownsville factory was producing a complete product line that was of very high quality. "The quality was so good that we used products directly from the factory for the show," Hampson said. "For years it had been standard industry practice to repaint and carefully detail units for shows." The new company's first dealer meeting was held later that year in Orlando, Florida. By then it had several new products to unveil.

Cub Cadet production models and model numbers remained unchanged for 1983, but there was some excitement toward the end of that year. Kubota gave Hampson a small 10-horsepower two-cylinder diesel engine at the GIA show early in 1983, and he brought it back to Cleveland in the trunk of his car and placed it in John McFadden's office. McFadden was then the president of both CCC and MTD. "It was a jewel of an engine, but we thought it was too small, so [Kubota] gave us a three-cylinder, 15-horsepower engine," Hampson said. The design team at CCC quickly fit the liquid-cooled engine into its garden tractor chassis and coupled it with a heavy-duty Sunstrand hydrostatic transmission. "Our biggest problem with that unit was fitting a big enough battery to light the engine's glow plugs, and then crank over the engine," Hampson said.

The team finally settled on a battery with more densely packed plates, but it was really marginal at best. Battery issues notwithstanding, within only a few months, the 782D was born, as CCC's first really new product.

"We made a big deal of the new 782D at the [1983] Orlando sales meeting," Hampson said. "John LaBoda [CCC's chief engineer] drove the tractor through a banner and into the meeting." The diesel-powered Cub Cadet had been tested extensively at the MTD farm in Valley City and had been put through its paces at Baldwin-Wallace College in Berea, Ohio.

When the 782D was released to IH dealers for the 1984 model year (along with all of the previous models), it was a big success, and it proved that the new company was capable of building on IH's strong Cub Cadet tradition. When released to CCC dealers alongside the previous year's models, the Model 782D wore the number 882 and was, of course, painted yellow and white.

On November 26, 1984, the seriously ailing International Harvester Company announced the sale of its Agricultural Equipment Division to Tenneco, Inc., of Houston, Texas. And while there was no immediate announcement of the fate of IH's ag dealers and no immediate plan to quit producing IH tractors (which continued until May 14, 1985), Herb Hampson and his team at CCC could see the writing on the wall. Tenneco's J. I. Case subsidiary had left the outdoor power products business in 1983 by selling to Ingersoll, and with Case and IH joining forces, Hampson was wise to be concerned with both the fate of a large proportion of his dealers and perhaps even more importantly the fate of the Cub Cadet parts distribution system.

At that point, CCC products were sold through about 1,000 IH ag dealers and 500 independent Cub Cadet dealers. By January 15, 1985, Herb and his team had put together a proposal to MTD for CCC to develop its own parts distribution system, which was implemented later that year. In fact, by May 1985, CCC was already handling a large portion of the parts orders. By September 1985, all of the warranty claims involving Cub Cadet machinery (both red and yellow and white) were being handled by CCC, and during that month, J. I. Case continued to ship semi loads of parts from the former IH depots to CCC headquarters near Cleveland.

Although IH's ag dealers received some Cub Cadet garden tractors in 1985 (the Model 1282 was dropped), it was really the end of the line for Cub Cadets bearing the IH insignia. In fact, some of the last red units produced were shipped without any IH decals because stock was depleted. As Tenneco sorted out the dealer network with its new Case-IH stores, Hampson's sales group saw a wonderful marketing opportunity that would benefit both CCC and the dealerships themselves. The team—

Deere and Company's Yanmar diesel-powered Model 332 is a real workhorse. This machine makes the plowing work short with its three-point hitch and Brinly plow.

This Yanmar diesel-powered Model 430 super garden tractor is hitched to a custom-fabricated two-bottom plow. It obviously has no problem pulling the implement through this tough Pennsylvania shale ground.

including Al DeSantis, Al Hersturm, and Bill Morris— traveled all over the United States holding Case-IH dealer meetings, and signed up many of them as Cub Cadet dealers.

By eliminating the highly protected IH ag distribution system, both CCC and the dealers enjoyed more attractive margins, and according to Hampson, CCC had its best year ever once the company was able to change its relationship with the former IH ag dealers.

At the time, CCC typically limited its long-term planning to one-year benchmarks. "With a very small engineering staff, and a small sales and marketing staff, we had a lot of balls to juggle and weren't thinking five years down the road," Hampson said. "We made an annual change or freshening of the product line; we made many minor changes to improve performance, correct a fault, or reduce cost."

The company's 1985 yellow-and-white garden tractor line included hydrostatic Models 1210, 1512, 1710, 1711, 1712, 1912, and 1914 with power ratings from 12 horsepower to 19.9 horsepower. Model 1512 was

powered with the liquid-cooled Kubota engine, and the 1912 and 1914 were direct descendents of the 984 and the 986 (later called super garden tractors).

Only two gear-drive garden tractors were available in 1985: the 1604, which utilized the Peerless four-speed transaxle and belt-idler clutch system on the 482, and the 1606, which utilized the three-speed sliding gear transmission descended from the Cub with the two-speed auxiliary creeper standard. Interestingly, the Cub Cadet Tractors brochure for 1985 used many of the same photographs as the 1984 catalog, but the model numbers on the tractors were blacked out; luckily, at that time the model number was located within the black field of the decal.

With International Harvester's long shadow and quirky distribution system now completely out of the picture, the team at CCC was finally able to look to an unencumbered future. The transition was finally over, and the company turned its focus to moving ahead.

In 1986, CCC offered a virtually unchanged tractor design, but the machines wore a new decal and logo. The new logo and look were clean and to the point. The

Rich Iowa bean ground is no match for the diesel-powered 430 hooked to a Brinly plow.

words "Cub Cadet," in an emblem with script lettering, were now located on either side of the Cub Cadet's hood, and the wedge-shaped black-and-blue decal was replaced by a clean series of black, yellow, and blue stripes. The look was very appealing, and it was much easier to read the model information on that decal than previously. The red-and-black CCC decal was used early in 1986, but later in the model year it was absent.

Gear-drive Models 1604 and 1606 were back in 1986, as were the hydrostatic Models 1210, 1512 Diesel, and larger-framed 1912 and 1914. New 18-horsepower hydrostatic Models 1810, 1811, and 1812 took the place of the 17-horsepower versions of the prior year. Hydraulic-assisted steering was now available on the 1512, 1811, 1812, 1912, and 1914, although it was an added-cost option. This was the last year for a diesel-powered tractor with the shorter garden tractor frame.

In 1987, gear-drive Models 1204 and 1806 replaced the 1604 and 1606 from the year prior. The 12-horsepower Model 1204 utilized the four-speed Peerless transaxle, while the 18-horsepower Model 1806 used the

three-speed transmission with two-speed auxiliary creeper. The 12-horsepower hydrostatic Model 1210 was back in 1987 and was joined by a new Model 1211 with hydraulic deck lift. Models 1810 and 1811 were also available in 1987. Perhaps the biggest changes in the Cub Cadet lineup for 1987 were naming the tractors with the longer frame Super Garden Tractors (SGT) and releasing three new models.

The new 20-horsepower SGT Model 2072 was available early in 1987, and the 18-horsepower Model 1872 SGT and liquid-cooled Kubota diesel-powered 1572 SGT quickly followed. As in the past, all of these larger-framed tractors used heavy-duty Sunstrand hydrostatic transmissions, and they now came standard with dual external brakes and dual brake-pedal control. Power steering was also now standard on these tractors.

The same Cub Cadet garden tractor models were available in 1988 as the previous year, except that the 12-horsepower 1204 was replaced with the 10-horsepower Model 1050; however, this tractor used the more robust three-speed sliding gear transmission rather than the four-

The 1980s vintage Model 316 tractors were powered with Onan engines, had single-function hydraulics, and lacked hydraulic oil coolers. This is an entry-level 300 Series machine. *Author's collection*

speed Peerless transaxle. In 1989, the diesel-powered Model 1772 SGT replaced the Model 1572. A larger 17-horsepower Kubota engine powered the 1772.

By 1989, CCC had survived the transition from IH and the negative feelings toward the brand because of IH's failure and MTD's involvement. The company had made small, steady improvements in a largely unchanged design, but it enjoyed a good reputation as a premium garden tractor brand. CCC had big plans for the last decade of the twentieth century, and they included a radical change in Cub Cadet styling that included composite materials and innovations in comfort, safety, and mowing technology. The company continues to innovate in the lawn and garden industry today.

John Deere

Deere & Company offered a full lineup of garden tractors in 1980—most carried over from the previous year. These included Models 210, 212, 214, and 216, all of

which remained in production until the end of the 1987 model year. These machines used the Vari-Speed belt-drive system and Peerless transaxle. Deere offered these as light-duty garden tractors that were especially suited to mowing and other easier chores.

The 300 Series garden tractors were also back for 1980 with Models 314 and 317. These 14-horsepower and 17-horsepower tractors remained relatively unchanged from 1979 through the 1983 model year, which is when the company released a completely redesigned Model 318. This tractor was equipped with an iso-mounted 18-horsepower twin-cylinder Onan engine, Tecumseh hydrostatic transmission, and hydrostatic power steering.

In 1984, the 318 was joined by a new Model 316 (not to be confused with the 1970s vintage 316), which was essentially a stripped-down 318 that offered only single-spool hydraulics and manual steering. In 1986, the Model 330 joined the team. This tractor was Deere's first diesel-powered garden tractor (it had a three-cylinder Yanmar unit). The 330 was replaced in 1988 with the 332. The Model 322 had a three-cylinder Yanmar gasoline engine. Several of these tractors survived into the 1990s.

In 1980, the massive Model 400 was John Deere's flagship garden tractor, but it was replaced in 1983 with a clean-sheet-designed Model 420. This super garden tractor was powered with a 20-horsepower twin-cylinder Onan engine and featured a heavier-duty axle, hydrostatic power steering, and updated styling, among other improvements. The hydrostatically driven machine even had an oil cooler to keep its life fluid at safe operating temperatures. In 1884, a Yanmar diesel-powered sibling known as the 430 joined the fleet. These big supers remained in Deere & Company's garden tractor lineup until the early 1990s, which is when the entire line was updated once again.

Deere's 318 remains one of the most sought-after garden tractors by collectors and by folks needing a good, workable machine. The company is still going strong in the outdoor power products arena and continues to offer a full line of lawn and garden equipment today.

Case and Ingersoll

In 1980, Tenneco's J. I. Case Company offered Models 210, 220, 222, 224, 444, and 446 as carryovers from the previous year. Added to the garden tractor lineup was the new Model 448. The 448 was very similar to the 446 except that it was powered with an 18-horsepower twin-cylinder Onan. Also in 1980, the front-end-loader-equipped Model 644 was dropped and the 18-horsepower Model 648 was added.

In 1981, Case's garden tractor lineup was virtually unchanged, except that the only wheel-loader tractor remaining was the 648. The 1982 and 1983 garden tractor offerings were identical to those available in 1981.

Looking to drop noncore businesses in the early 1980s, Case's parent company, Tenneco, decided to liquidate its Outdoor Power Equipment Division (still located in Winneconne, Wisconsin) in 1983. By the end of that year, the division was sold to Jack S. Ingersoll (a relative to the family involved with Ingersoll-Rand) with the stipulation that he would continue to supply Case dealerships with Case-branded equipment. This

Case's Model 648 loader tractor was designed to move materials, but it could also power a belly-mounted mower or rear-mounted rotary tiller. *Author's collection*

This 1983 Case 448 was among the last to be built by Case. The next year's models were actually built by Ingersoll, even though they were essentially identical.

Ingersoll's Model 448 was initially sold with both Case and Ingersoll branding. By 1986, however, the Case name was dropped. *Author's collection*

Ingersoll continued to make the 600 Series loader tractors in the 1980s. It offered the 648 HyLoad loader and 648 HyLoad loader/backhoe.

practice was maintained until 1986, when Tenneco pulled the plug on corporate-branded outdoor power equipment altogether. Ingersoll-branded garden tractors were available at some Case dealerships at that point, but others (former IH dealers) often already carried the Cub Cadet brand.

In 1984, a 16-horsepower Model 226 was released. The Ingersoll/Case garden tractor lineup through 1988 included Models 210, 220, 222, 224, 226, 444, 446, 448, and 648. By the end of the century, Ingersoll had revamped, renamed, and refocused the line. Diesel power was part of that mix, along with better, safer machines.

In 1990, Ingersoll was sold to the Rothenberger group, a German outfit. In 1991, the company purchased M&W Gear's Grazer mower line and produced zero-turning-radius mowers under that and the Ingersoll names. Today, Ingersoll is located in Portland, Maine, as a subsidiary of the Eastman Group. Robust garden tractors are still part of the lineup.

Bolens

In 1980, the Bolens garden tractor lineup included a vast array of light-, heavy-, and super-duty models. Models included the 11-horsepower G11XL, the 12-horsepower gear and hydrostatic Models G12XL and H12XL, the 14-horsepower gear and hydro Models G14XL and H14XL,

By the late 1980s, the Bolens Model GT1800 was powered with a Kohler 18-horsepower twin-cylinder engine and featured an Eaton hydrostatic transmission and a Bolen's final drive.

the 16-horsepower gear-drive G16XL, the 17-horsepower Kohler-powered hydro QT17, the 18-horsepower hydro H18XL, the 20-horsepower diesel hydro HT20D and HT22, the 23-horsepower hydro HT23, the 15-horsepower twin-cylinder Mitsubishi diesel gear-drive G152 and G154, the 17-horsepower twin-cylinder Mitsubishi diesel–powered gear-drive G172 and G174, and four Isuzu diesel–powered compact tractors—two rated at 19 horsepower and two at 24 horsepower.

This plethora of models was the norm at Bolens for the next several years as the company continued to offer several different combinations of engines and transmissions in various chassis. This trend continued throughout the 1980s and into the early 1990s. In 1989, the largest Bolens tractor was rated at 27 horsepower with Isuzu diesel power and an 18-speed transmission.

After ownership by Garden Way Inc. in the late 1980s, MTD agreed to purchase holding company Bolens and Troy-Bilt assets for more than $40 million. The Bolens name went out of production for a few years, but

MTD brought it back in the early 2000s to represent a line of lawn and garden products sold exclusively through Lowe's Home Improvement Warehouse.

Vintage Bolens machinery remains highly collectible, and many owners cherish time spent maintaining their property with the well-built machines.

Jacobsen

In 1980, Jacobsen's garden tractor lineup included 10- and 12-horsepower gear-driven Models 1000 and 1200. Both were powered with single-cylinder Kohler engines and offered four forward speeds with one reverse; optional electric lift was available in place of manual lift. That same year, the company offered a trio of Kohler-powered hydrostats with 12-, 14- and 16-horsepower engines—the 1250, 1450, and 1650. The mechanical lift was standard on the 1250, while one or two spool hydraulics (including lift) were optional. The higher-horsepower hydros offered single-spool hydraulic lift as standard.

Jacobsen also offered its Heavy Duty Tractor that same year. This machine was powered with a 19.5-horsepower Kohler twin-cylinder engine and offered a dual-range hydrostatic transmission. The Heavy Duty was right in line with other super garden tractors of the day and came standard with two-spool hydraulics. A Category 0 three-point hitch was optional.

Jacobsen garden tractors were offered through the decade, but in the 1990s, its parent company, Textron Inc., sold the line. Some references indicate that the sale went directly to John Deere in 1994. Obviously, Deere and Company had no need for the Jacobsen garden tractor lineup, but it was able to pick up a good set of smaller outdoor power products in the process. In 2001, John Deere sold Homelite to an Asian group.

Speedex

In 1980, Speedex added a 16-horsepower Briggs & Stratton–powered hydrostatic transmission Model 16H (1622 Hydro) to the lineup that also included the 1040, 1240, 1630, 1631, and 1632. The 16H was rated for a single eight-inch-wide moldboard plow and featured the same no-frills styling of its siblings. It was also equipped with the Category 0 three-point hitch and hydraulic lift.

By 1984, some 16-horsepower models were still available in a slightly more styled version. That same year, the company also had an 18-horsepower big garden tractor

that was patterned after the older style with round headlights. This Model 1832-3000 was equipped with a T-92 three-speed automotive-style transmission and offered hydraulic lift.

In 1986, the lineup included completely restyled models such as the 1640, whose most striking features were the new fiberglass fenders, grille, and hood. The machine was powered with a twin-cylinder Briggs & Stratton Vanguard engine, rated at 16 horsepower.

By the end of the decade, Speedex tractors had lost their familiar red color in favor of beige with orange accents (it almost looked like a Case tractor). These tractors, called the Falcon Series, came in 16- and 18-horsepower versions. They were available with four-speed transmissions or hydros. Speedex production continued until 1998 and included several noteworthy models, such as the large-framed 16-horsepower 1631 diesel and truly futuristic-looking 20-horsepower Model 2032.

Today, Speedex enjoys some of the most loyal collectors, who enjoy tinkering with, using, and showing these robust little machines.

Kubota's Model G2160 offers unprecedented operator comfort and safety in an efficient diesel-powered package that's hard to beat in the twenty-first century. *Author's collection*

This original condition Speedex Model 1632 still has plenty of working life left in it.

Engineering Products Co. Power King

Power King history gets a little sparse in the 1980s. The maker was still active and produced several models, ranging from 14 to 18 horsepower on two chassis with variously sized tires. In 1982, the 1614, 2414, 1618, 2418, 1616, and 2416 all received a four-speed transmission. Earlier that year, the Jim Dandy–derived line was redesigned to include bodywork constructed of composite materials (plastics). These tractors, which comprised the 1200 Series, were initially all gear driven, but sometime in 1983, hydrostatic transmissions became available also. In 1984, the large chassis 1614, 1617, 2414, and 2417, as well as the 1600 and 2400 Series tractors, followed suit with the new styling.

In 1990, Engineering Products became a subsidiary of Support Services, Inc. The company produced tractors at least through the late 1990s.

Gravely

Gravely's 8000 Series riding garden tractors were still available in 1980 and the lineup was virtually unchanged from the year before. In 1985, the models carried a "G" suffix

Wheel Horse's C Series machines were a little more robust than the B Series. This C-195 is equipped with a 60-inch mowing deck. *Author's collection*

and included the 8199-G, 8179-G, 8163-G, 8123-G, and 8122-G. Just like their predecessors, they were powered with engines ranging from 12 to about 19 horsepower.

In 1988, the 8000 Series garden tractors were replaced with the Professional G tractors. These machines used the same eight-speed transaxle as the 8000 Series, but they had increased power options and other changes to the lineup. In that first year, the Professional G lineup included the 12-G, 16-G, 18-G, and 20-G. The number indicates the tractor's horsepower. Engine makers included Onan, Kohler, and Briggs & Stratton.

Ariens purchased Gravely in 1982 and has been operating the brand as a wholly owned subsidiary ever since. No longer in the garden tractor–making business, Gravely continues to build quality zero-turning-radius mowers and other equipment.

Wheel Horse

Numerous Wheel Horse garden tractors were offered into the 1980s. Engine power ranged widely, and drivetrains included five-speed and eight-speed gear transmissions, as well as hydrostats. In 1985, Toro purchased Wheel Horse, and the company still offers some models bearing the Wheel Horse name.

Simplicity

In 1980, Simplicity's garden tractor lineup included the bulk of the company's 1979 offerings with a few additions. Other models included the small-frame 6108, 6111, 6116, and 6118 with manual lift. These tractors evolved through the 6200 and 6500 Series and into the GT Series by 1991. Large-frame 7100 Series tractors available in 1980 included the 7110, 7112, 7114, 7116, and 7117 with manual lift. By 1982, an 18.5-horsepower (19 horsepower in some references) Model 7790 two-cylinder diesel was available, and the 6100 Series had evolved into the 6200 Series.

The 6200 Series included Models 6211, 6216, and 6218 in 1982, and these tractors continued evolving well

The 500 Series super garden tractors were among Wheel Horse's largest and most powerful machines. They were typically marketed to maintenance firms and large estate owners. *Author's collection*

beyond the decade. In 1987, the Sunstar (GTH) line of larger super garden tractors was introduced.

Simplicity tractors are still in production as part of the Briggs & Stratton Power Products Group, LLC program.

Special Duty and Allied Equipment

The list of approved allied equipment for various garden tractor makes is staggering and includes many different types of mowers, tillers, graders, golf-course tools, loaders, cultivators, aerators, cabs, baggers, fertilizer spreaders, sweepers, backhoes, planters, rollers, toolbars, etc. There are fewer manufacturers of allied equipment than the number of pieces themselves, but even that list is long. And then there are numerous makers of pull-type tools that were never formally approved by tractor manufacturers; these makers produce many additional useful implements that made the possibilities with a garden tractor virtually unlimited.

In 1984, Wheel Horse's 16-horsepower B-165 automatic tractor was a perfect match for the company's 30-inch tiller. *Author's collection*

ABOVE: Simplicity's Model 7116 was among the large-frame offerings in the early 1980s. This tractor has hydraulic lift and hydrostatic drive.

MIDDLE: A close-up of Simplicity's Model 7116 grille decal.

BOTTOM: Simplicity's twenty-first-century garden tractor offerings include a lineup of powerful diesels with four-wheel drive and dual-pedal hydrostatic transmission control. *Author's collection*

Mowers

Garden tractor owners had an overwhelming choice of mowers for use with their tractors, in addition to the mower decks often sold as part of the initial package. Examples include the triple-gang pull-type reel mower attachments from Yardman of Jackson, Michigan, Pennsylvania Brand (American Chain and Cable Company of Exeter, Pennsylvania), and Turfmaster (Dille & McGuire Manufacturing Company of Richmond, Indiana). These reel mowers were designed for or adapted

TORO

The Toro Motor Company was founded in Minneapolis, Minnesota, in 1914 and was initially set up to manufacture and machine components for the Bull Tractor Company. When Bull Tractor went out of business in 1918, Toro pushed on, eventually becoming the Toro Manufacturing Company. By 1920, Toro offered a two-row motor cultivator that could also be used for some drawbar work. This machine never caught on in a big way, and it was overshadowed by agricultural giant International Harvester's efforts with the Farmall tractor.

The company redefined itself as a turf-maintenance manufacturer in the early 1920s, when it was approached by an exclusive country club looking for a specialized tractor for pulling reel-type lawn mowers. By 1925, Toro's greens cutting machines had taken the golfing industry by storm. Most good courses used Toro equipment, and virtually all greens keepers wanted it. Further early developments in the finish mower realm included self-propelled walk-behind greens cutters, as well as larger, gentler tractor-powered units.

Toro Manufacturing of Minnesota, as it was renamed in 1935, was sold after World War II to David Lilly, Bob Gibson, and Whit Miller, and the company rapidly expanded into consumer markets with its Sportlawn reel-type mower and a whole family of powered rotary mowers. These came about as the result of Toro's acquisition of Whirlwind, a Milwaukee-based maker. In

little time, Toro was making mowers, snow throwers, grass-bagging equipment, and many other products to help suburban dwellers get the most of their properties.

In the 1960s, Toro expanded its golf and homeowner offerings and added turf irrigation products as well. The company released the industry's first electric-start walk-behind lawn mower in 1968, and a trio of garden tractors came on line in 1967. These little tractors were all powered with Kohler engines, featured gear-drive transaxles, and came in 8-, 10-, and 12-horsepower versions. Although garden tractors were never a huge part of Toro's bottom line, they have had a presence in the company's offerings from the late 1960s to the present.

In the 1970s, Toro's sales grew phenomenally. The growth was driven in part by expanded offerings of snow blowers, mowers, and more. The company moved away from dealer marketing to mass merchandising in the 1980s, which hurt the brand's reputation somewhat, but top execs hoped that the increased volume of sales would make up for the lower profit per unit.

Toro purchased Wheel Horse in 1986, which overnight made the company into a significant garden tractor player. Today, Toro markets garden tractors with the Wheel Horse name on them.

to specific tractors and could be used by golf courses, sports complexes, or homeowners to get that carefully manicured look with 57-inch to 87-inch swaths.

Later equipment catalogs show reel mowers offered by the same makers in gang numbers up to five. Most were still pull-type, although Roxy-Bonner (Roxy-Bonner Manufacturing Inc. of Huntingdon Valley, Pennsylvania) offered a three-reel gang with two of the reels mounted on the front of the tractor and one behind. More recent catalogs feature triple-gang pull-type reel mowers from Agri-Fab of Sullivan, Illinois.

The early equipment catalogs also feature Mott

(Mott Corporation of La Grange, Illinois) hammer knife (flail) mowers for use with specific garden tractor models. In the case of the Cub Cadet, 32-inch-cut mowers were mounted on the front of the tractors. One was powered by the Cub Cadet's engine, while the other had its own 5.5-horsepower engine. The third model was a self-powered trailing mower that could also be gang hitched for a wider swath. The trailing-type self-powered Mott mowers are easy to adapt to virtually any garden tractor simply by hitching them up.

Haban Manufacturing Company of Racine, Wisconsin, also offered flail mowers that mounted to the

Snapper-branded machines are available with powerful diesel engines (the 27-horsepower model is shown here), true ground-engaging ability, and four-wheel drive. This so-called subcompact tractor can even be equipped with a loader.

Ariens yard tractors could be equipped with a 36-inch-wide two-stage snow thrower in the early 1980s. *Author's collection*

front of various garden tractor makes and models. The Haban flail mower had a 36-inch cut. By the 1980s, Haban also offered a 48-inch and 60-inch rear-mounted flail mower designed to be mounted on a super garden tractor's Category 0 three-point hitch, powered by a rear PTO.

Sickle bar mowers built by the Haban Manufacturing Company were also available. Initially, they were mounted between the front and rear wheels, were powered by the tractor's front PTO, and cut a 48-inch swath. Later, Haban offered a rear-mounted sickle bar mower for super garden tractors equipped with the Category 0 three-point hitch and rear PTO. The Jiffy-Balling Company of Rockford, Minnesota, produced a front-mounted sickle bar mower for several makers, including Wheel Horse and Cub Cadet. It was available in either a 36-inch or 42-inch width. Didier Manufacturing of Racine, Wisconsin, also offered the Hydra-Sickle, a hydraulically driven side-mounted sickle bar mower for tractors with a PTO suitable for running a hydraulic pump.

Front- and rear-mounted rotary mowers were also available from at least two manufacturers over the years: Haban and Woods Manufacturing Company. These mowers were typically designed as finish mowers. Garden-tractor-sized rear-mounted rotary cutters have been offered by Bush Hog as well.

Sweepers and Vacuums

Sweeping and vacuuming attachments have been offered in some form from relatively early in the modern garden tractor era, but until quite recently the majority of those options were supplied by approved manufacturers. For example, Lambert Manufacturing Company's pull-type wheel-powered lawn sweeper was listed in the special duty catalog that accompanied the 1961 Cub Cadet along with a front-PTO-powered Jenkins Rotary Sweeper (made by Sweepster, Inc., of Dexter, Michigan). Sweepster's sweeper continues to be a highly sought attachment because of its utility and rarity.

Later catalogs listed wheel-powered, pull-type, single lawn sweepers by Lambert and Parker Sweeper

Company of Springfield, Ohio, and a triple-gang unit by Parker that offered a 100-inch sweep with a 48-bushel capacity for clippings or leaves. Along with the Sweepster front-mounted rotary broom, a self-powered pull-type Jenkins Pickup Sweeper was listed with a 48-inch sweeping width and either a four-bushel-capacity steel hopper or optional 23-bushel canvas hopper. The Pickup Sweeper was powered by its own four-horsepower gasoline engine and could be used on pavement or turf.

By the 1970s, powered rotary broom sweepers were also available from Mars Industries, Inc., of Minneapolis, Minnesota. These competed directly with the Jenkins Sweepster units. The front-mounted Mars Rotary Sweeper utilized a 44-inch-wide broom that could be angled left or right and was powered by its own 3.5-horsepower gasoline engine. The self-powered Mars pull-type Pick-Up Sweeper was available with either a 7-cubic-foot- or 20-cubic-foot-capacity hopper.

Lawn vacuums were typically mounted on a garden tractor's drawbar or on a cart and were powered with their own engine. Most of these devices were plumbed directly to the mower deck's discharge chute. Early versions of

In 1988, Outboard Marine Corporation's Lawn Boy division offered the GT18H, which was a fully equipped hydrostatically driven garden tractor. It even came with a Category 0 three-point hitch. *Author's collection*

Mitsubishi's Satoh Beaver is very similar to some of the subcompact diesels that Bolens offered. This particular machine has 16.5-horsepower engine, four-wheel drive, and a dual-range eight-speed sliding spur-gear transmission. *Author's collection*

vacuum sweepers were supplied by E-Z-Rake, Inc., of Lebanon, Indiana. Later versions came from JRCO, Inc., of Minneapolis, Minnesota, and PeCo, Inc., of Arden, North Carolina. Small pull-type, self-powered floor or pavement vacuums that look like small street sweepers were also available from Lambert.

Recent lawn sweeper and vacuum offerings include several models produced by Agri-Fab.

Other Turf Care Tools

The following list is by no means exhaustive, but it gives an indication of the number of manufacturers who made rollers, aerators, seeders, fertilizer spreaders, rakes, and other tools that were approved for use with various garden tractors to maintain and renovate turf. Catalogs from the 1960s and 1970s list pull-type lawn rollers being produced by Kensico Manufacturing Company (of Mount Kisco, New York), Greenlawn Aerators, Inc. (of Greenville, Pennsylvania), Ohio Steel Fabricators (of Columbus, Ohio), and Harris Fabricating Company (of Youngstown, Ohio). Later catalogs retain the Kensico and Ohio Steel Fabricators models and have the Rol-Aerator models from the Brinly-Hardy Company (of Louisville, Kentucky) listed. Today, Agri-Fab continues to offer many different rollers.

Early pull-type spiker-aerators were supplied by makers such as Kensico, Brinly-Hardy, Ohio Steel Fabricators, Gill Manufacturing Company (of Charlotte, North Carolina), Harris Manufacturing Company (of Youngstown, Ohio), Agri-Fab, and others. Plug-type aerators were available from Greenlawn, Brinly-Hardy, and Agri-Fab.

Rakes and other thatching tools were also listed among the approved Special Duty and Allied Equipment. For example, Robbie Rake's lawn rake for thatching and debris collection was listed as early as late 1961. Later, Brinly-Hardy offered a compactor rake that could loosen thatch and collect it in plastic refuse bags, a reusable bag, or a canvas hopper. E-Z-Rake offered a pair of front-mount thatchers in the late 1960s, each with a 37.5-inch raking width. One was powered from the tractor's

In the mid-1980s, Ford offered a complete lineup of lawn and garden equipment, including this 18-horsepower LGT-18H yard tractor. *Author's collection*

front PTO and the other was equipped with its own four-horsepower gasoline engine. Later, pull-type tine thatchers (sometimes called de-thatchers) were available from Brinly-Hardy and Agri-Fab.

Over the years, drop-type lawn seeders and fertilizer spreaders have been available from many different manufacturers, such as Viking Manufacturing Company (of Manhattan, Kansas), Schneider Metal Manufacturing Company (of Chicago, Illinois), Parker Sweeper Company (of Springfield, Ohio), Gandy Company (of Owatonna, Minnesota), and Agri-Fab. All of these models were designed to be pulled by the tractor and had adjustable gates and agitators powered directly off the wheels.

Spinner-type broadcast spreaders were available in either wheel-driven or 12-volt motor-driven models, depending on the manufacturer. For example, Brinly-Hardy offered a 100-pound-capacity broadcast spreader that mounted on the tractor's hitch plate with an electric motor–powered spinner and a similar capacity pull-type model with spinner power coming from the wheels. Cyclone Seeder Company of Urbana, Illinois, offered homeowner and commercial trailing broadcast spreaders with balloon tires, terra-tires, and an electrically operated front-mount unit. Central Quality Industries, Inc.,

The Viking Roller Blade was designed to plant or repair lawns and putting greens.

of Polo, Illinois, offered the trailing wheel-driven Roto Spreader-Seeder, and several of Agri-Fab's trailing broadcast spreaders were also approved allied equipment.

Sprayers and Foggers

Believe it or not, but spraying apparatuses also were available from a number of different manufacturers relatively early on. The H. D. Hudson Manufacturing Company of Chicago, Illinois—longtime makers of sprayers—offered a 2.5-gallon-capacity model that mounted on the tractor's hitch in the 1960s and 1970s. This sprayer was pressurized by its own engine-driven pump and could also be purchased as a trailing model. At the same time, the A. E. MacKissic Company of Parker Ford, Pennsylvania, offered a front-mounted sprayer that was powered by the front PTO of the tractor. The optional spray boom was mounted on the tractor's rear hitch.

In later years, Hudson sprayers continued to be offered, along with trailing-type Mighty Mac sprayers from Amerind-MacKissic, Inc. (formerly MacKissic Company, of Parker Ford, Pennsylvania), and rear-mounted sprayers from Mars. Agri-Fab also had several trailing sprayers on the allied equipment list.

In the 1960s, thermo-foggers were also on the allied equipment list. These tools typically used engine exhaust to vaporize and deliver an oil-based insecticide. For example, the Thermo-Fogger built by Burgess Vibrocrafters, Inc., of Grayslake, Illinois, and the Blitz Fogger produced by Northern Industries, Inc., of Milwaukee, Wisconsin, both worked on the same principle. The simple Blitz Fogger consisted of an insecticide tank mounted on the tractor's hood and a neoprene line connecting the tank with an injector tapped into the tractor's muffler. When the valve was opened, the insecticide flowed into the hot muffler, creating a thick, poisonous fog—right in front of the operator. The Thermo-Fogger unit was mounted at the rear on the tractor's drawbar and had its own three-horsepower engine. In either case, the operator was likely exposed to a great deal of insecticide when using the fogger.

Landscaping Tools

From the very beginning, four-wheel garden tractors were useful for doing light earth-moving and grading work. Many could be equipped with a 300-pound-capacity Danco front-end loader that came complete with its own hydraulic system run from the tractor's front PTO. Likewise, a tractor could be fit with a 42-inch center-mounted grader blade built by the Covina Equipment Company of Irwindale, California.

In time, other loaders became available from the Johnson Hydraulic Equipment Company (of Minneapolis, Minnesota), Schwartz Products Company (of Lester

Golfing had so captivated the suburban mind by the late 1960s that IH offered a special sand trap rake that could be matched with a dual-tire-equipped Cub Cadet to make smoothing the area easier.

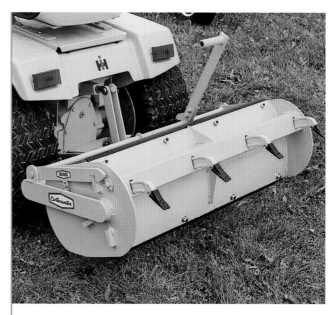

Gannon's little Earthcavator fit nicely on the standard garden tractor's hitch. The innovative little scraper/roll pan was lever operated.

Prairie, Minnesota), and K-W (Kwik-Way) Manufacturing Company (of Sioux Falls, South Dakota). The loaders were generally self-contained, complete with pump and reservoir. Center-mounted grader blades were also available from Johnson and A. B. Daly & Company of Coos Bay, Oregon. York Modern Corporation of Unadilla, New York, manufactured rear-mounted and trailing grader blades and landscape rakes for the Cub Cadet and many other garden tractors. Small rear grader blades and box blades were available from Brinly-Hardy, Agri-Fab, Gannon Manufacturing Inc. (of Buena Park, California), and others.

Perhaps one of the most interesting and unusual earth-moving implements designed for heavier garden tractors is the Soil Mover Corporation's 9-cubic-foot-capacity, 36-inch-cut hydraulic pan scraper. This mini-scraper could also be converted into a cart with the installation of a removable panel at the front of the pan.

If you needed to drill holes in the ground for fence posts or transplants, Danuser Machine Company of Fulton, Missouri, produced the Hole Digger rear-mounted attachment for some garden tractors. This augur-type

post-hole digger employed a hydraulic powerhead to turn the drill and could make holes from 4 inches to 14 inches in diameter. If holes weren't your thing, but you had some water or electric lines to trench in, the Hawk-Bilt Corporation's rear-mounted Groundsaw Trencher was available. The little hydraulically powered trencher could dig 36 inches deep in widths from 2.25 to 6 inches.

Gardening Tools

As a heavy-duty gardening tool, a good garden tractor supplied power for attachments capable of performing every task. From working the soil to planting to shredding the season's leftovers, some piece of special duty or allied equipment could get the job done.

Early spring or late fall plowing could be readily accomplished with a single-bottom moldboard plow attached to the tractor's rear hitch. Mounted single-bottom land plows with 8-inch, 10-inch, and 12-inch shares have been available from Brinly-Hardy throughout the lifespan of most garden tractors. Companies like Brinly-Hardy, Planet Jr. (made by S. L. Allen Company Inc. of Philadelphia, Pennsylvania), and Agri-Fab offered single- and double-gang disc harrows, spike-tooth

Wheel Horse offered a front-mount sickle bar mower for its tractors. Jiffy-Balling offered similar models for many different makes of tractors.

harrows, and spring-tine harrows. Fuerst Brothers, Inc., of Oregon, Illinois, produced tine harrows for both seedbed preparation and ball diamond grooming, and Brinly-Hardy also offered a Rolling Spike smoothing harrow for final seedbed preparation.

Once the seedbed was prepared, the gardener needed only choose a one-row or two-row planter from makers such as Planet Jr. and Brinly-Hardy to put the crop in (Brinly-Hardy's planter was made to specification by Cole Manufacturing Company). Single-row cultivators offered by Brinly-Hardy, Planet Jr., and Agri-Fab made it easy to keep the weeds down during the growing season, or at least until the crop canopied. Once the harvest was over, a MacKissic (later Amerind-MacKissic) front- or rear-mount PTO-driven Chipper-Shredder came in handy.

For those who preferred the soil pulverizing action of a rotary tiller, Planet Jr.'s rear-mounted, self-powered unit was available in the 1960s and 1970s. Agri-Fab offered tillers later. Of course, many tractor manufacturers offered their own tillers, but another company often built them.

Miscellaneous Attachments

Although there really wasn't much in the way of comfort-related allied equipment for most garden tractors, several cabs and shades were available. Snow Company of Omaha, Nebraska, made a Sun-Brella umbrella available in colors to match virtually any brand. Canvas or vinyl-coated canvas cabs were available from makers such as Sims Cabs, Inc., of Rutland, Massachusetts. These weather protectors typically had a sheet-metal roof and frame with a glass windshield and clear-vinyl side and rear windows that snapped into place along with the rest of the fabric; however, Sims produced several all-steel cabs, too. Custom Products of Litchfield, Inc. (of Litchfield, Minnesota), offered its all-metal-and-glass All-Weather Cozy Cab for many garden tractor models, as well. The Original Tractor Cab Company of Arlington, Indiana, continues to produce shades and soft-sided cabs for various machines.

In the event that an owner wished to use his or her garden tractor as a portable electrical power source, several front-mounted PTO-driven power-generating devices were available. For example, at least five different Pincor brand (made by Pioneer Gen-E-Motor Corporation of Chicago, Illinois) quick-attach generators were available with output capacities from 1,000 to 3,500 watts. These units were equipped with a power inverter and either 115-volt or 230-volt AC outlets. If generating AC current was your primary requirement, Generac brand alternators (made by General Corporation of Waukesha, Wisconsin) were available with 2,000-watt and 4,000-watt capacities.

Pincor made all kinds of garden-tractor compatible generators. This one is mounted on a Cub Cadet Corporation–built Model 982.

For the golf course operator, Wittek Golf Range Supply Company, Inc. (of Chicago, Illinois), offered a front-mounted golf ball retriever that could be optionally expanded from 3.5 feet to about 18 feet in width. For the golfer, Jenkins produced the fiberglass Sweepster-brand Golfer attachment that replaced the tractor's rear fenders and seat with a pair of comfortably upholstered seats and room in back for golf bags. The Golfer was also marketed as a utility carryall for transporting people, tools, parts, etc., around a manufacturing plant. As a golf cart or utility transporter, the Sweepster Golfer attachment is an extremely rare piece to find.

Collecting garden tractor attachments is another way to enjoy your vintage tractor. And in many cases, the implements and attachments are substantially more rare, as they are often more difficult to find than the tractors that powered them.

Brinly's Rolaerator is an unusual garden tractor implement that includes aerating blades directly in front of the roller.

Sprayer — HUDSON

Compact 12½-gallon capacity, engine powered sprayer mounts on back of Cub Cadet tractor. 1½-gpm pump develops up to 150 psi. Complete with 20-ft. Spray-Proof hose and adjustable power gun. 50-gallon capacity, trailing type sprayer also available.

Manufactured by H. D. HUDSON MANUFACTURING CO.
589 East Illinois Street, Chicago 11, Illinois
Order MODEL No. 12255
For Trailing Model, Order MODEL No. 35050
Trailer Hitch, No. 5950
4 Ft. Weed Boom, No. 1049A

Sprayer — MACKISSIC

15-gallon capacity front-mounted sprayer, driven by tractor front pto. 300 lb. maximum pressure, sprays distances up to 35 ft. with spray gun. Boom sprayer optional. Handles any sprayable material. Tank interior coated to prevent corrosion. Adjustable nozzle, pressure control valve. 25 ft. of hose with spray gun.

Manufactured by A. E. MACKISSIC COMPANY
Parker Ford, Pennsylvania
Order MODEL No. CC-E

Loader — DANCO

Lifts 300-lb. loads. 50-in. lift height. Raised and lowered hydraulically by two single-acting lift cylinders. 3 gpm front-mounted hydraulic pump.
All-welded, formed steel box construction. Automatic bucket lock. 150-pound rear counterweight recommended. Weight, 300 lb. approx.

Manufactured by DANUSER MACHINE WORKS, INC.
P.O. Box 5095, Tulsa, Oklahoma
Order MODEL No. RD-300

Blade — COVINA

42-inch wide, 6-inch high, blade is center-mounted under the Cub Cadet, and is controlled by the tractor's implement lift lever. The blade can be angled manually to the right or to the left, and can be tilted down at either end.

Manufactured by COVINA EQUIPMENT COMPANY
Irwindale, California   Order Model 161

Sprayers, loaders, and graders were all part of the Allied Equipment list for the Cub Cadet shortly after it was released in 1961. Similar lists applied to virtually every garden tractor brand out there. *Author's collection*